995

MW00795911

THE MAGNIFICENT NUMBERS
OF THE GREAT PYRAMID AND STONEHENGE

THE MAGNIFICENT NUMBERS
OF
THE GREAT PYRAMID
AND
STONEHENGE

These two ancient wonders
reveal their long-kept secrets
by the correlation of their magnificent numbers
—the numbers of the universe!

by BONNIE GAUNT

First Printing – 1985
Second Printing – 1988
Third Printing – 1996

For more information, write to
Bonnie Gaunt, 510 Golf Avenue, Jackson, Michigan 49203

Manufactured in the United States of America

ISBN 0-9602688-1-2

Library of Congress Card No. 85-091026

Dedicated
to
Dr. J. David Wood
founder of
The Village Church
The Village Academy
Institute of Aquaculture
Ark Park

Cedar Key Plantation
Cedar Key, Florida

for
his encouragement and
excitement in the study of
the Great Pyramid
and
Stonehenge

Foreword

Numbers have long been a source of fascination and wonder to man. The ancient Pythagoras was so awed by the relationship of numbers to time and space that he theorized: "Numbers are the language of the universe." And indeed Pythagoras was right.

The discovery of the inter-relationships of the numbers involved in the geometry of the Great Pyramid and Stonehenge led to a comprehensive investigation into the "language of the universe," and a glimpse into the very foundation of creation. The numbers reveal the evidence of the existence of an intelligent Creator.

This work has only scratched the surface of a subject too vast for the human mind fully to grasp. Yet it uncovers the unmistakable evidence of a consistent plan—a plan involving the destiny of the human race.

Come with me on a fascinating journey through time and space to discover the language of the universe—the magnificent numbers.

Bonnie Gaunt

Contents

*Science is not the solving
of problems so much as it is an
encounter with mysteries
which are less to be solved
than they are to
be revered*

1

The Oldest Wonder!

On the rocky plateau of Gizeh, fifteen miles from Cairo, stands the worlds most amazing wonder, the Great Pyramid. It stands silent and serene against the Egyptian sky, yet it stands in bold defiance against time; it stands as a sacred memorial to the intelligence of its builders, and to their knowledge of time, space, and the universe. The awesome grandeur of this magnificent structure commands our reverence. Its very mass boggles the mind. As we stand in its shadow and look upward we feel humbled and dwarfed by its enormity.

This only remaining wonder of the ancient world is also a wonder to the modern world. Its base covers thirteen acres. It contains enough masonry to build a sidewalk three inches thick and two feet wide around the world. It rises to a height comparable to a 40-story building that would fill seven blocks of midtown Manhattan. Built of solid limestone masonry throughout, except for its chambers and passage systems, clearly, whoever built the Great Pyramid wanted it to remain. And remain it has!

Each new generation of man has marveled at its construction and searched for its purpose. This ancient wonder has become a modern mystery.

The Great Pyramid was once covered with dazzling white casing stones which could be seen from great distances because it captured and reflected the sun's rays. The ancient Strabo said it was "like a building let down from heaven, untouched by human hands."

Theory has it that the great topstone was covered with gold. I can think of no better words to describe this magnificant monument than those written by Adam Rutherford.[1]

> ...what a Top-Stone! Think of its gigantic size, its tremendous weight and the fabulous cost of the gold to cover such a colossal Crowning Stone! Picture, in the brilliant sunshine, this great Top-Stone, arrayed in gold, in itself a perfect Pyramid of dazzling brilliance, towering high on the lofty summit of the massive Pyramid of snowy white—supreme magnificence indeed...!

Rutherford, however, was only creating a beautiful picture in the mind, because he elsewhere stated that this beautiful topstone had never been placed.[2] And the ancient writers who have described the Pyramid stated that it rose to a flat platform at the top. The classical writer Diodorus Siculus, who had seen the Great Pyramid before vandals had stripped it of its white casing stones, said that it tapered to a small square summit.

The workmanship of the builders of the Great Pyramid was without peer, even to modern times. The stones, some of which weighed as much as 50 tons, were cut to an accuracy within 1/50 of an inch. The mortar between the stones was so thin it can scarcely be detected with the naked eye, yet it was so strong that even after 4,000 years of the ravages of sun, rain and man the stones themselves will shatter before the mortar will yield.

Herodotus, who has been called "the father of history," saw the Great Pyramid in 440 B.C. By that time the structure would have been about 1,700 years old; however he said that each side of the Pyramid was covered with highly polished white limestone, with joints so fine they could scarcely be seen.

Strabo, who visited the Great Pyramid in 24 B.C., described a small opening on its north face, covered by a hinged stone

---

[1] Adam Rutherford, *Pyramidology Book II*, Institute of Pyramidology, London, 1962, p. 259.

[2] *Ibid.*, p. 233.

which could be raised, but would become indistinguishable from the surrounding masonry when closed. In later years the precise location of this door was lost, and the entire structure remained sealed until A.D. 820, when an opening was forced through the massive limestone by Al Mamoun.

Caliph Al Mamoun, who came to the throne in A.D. 813, had transformed Baghdad into a center of academic learning, including an astronomical observatory. He was an accomplished astronomer and had been responsible for the translating of Ptolemy's *Almagest* into Arabic. His interest in astronomy led him to the Great Pyramid, for he had been informed that it contained a secret chamber with maps and tables of the celestial sphere.

In the year A.D. 820 Al Mamoun employed a vast number of architects, engineers and stone masons, in the hope of entering the Great Pyramid and finding its treasures. For days they searched the north face for the mysterious secret door, but without success. No trace of it could be found. Knowing that its entrance was on the north face, and hence that its passage system originated there, he decided to force his way in through the solid limestone.

His men soon found that hammer and chisel were to no avail—they could not penetrate the strength of those huge limestone blocks. So a more scientific method was employed. They built fires close to the limestone blocks, and when they became red hot, they would pour cold vinegar over them until they cracked. The fragmented stones were then knocked loose by the use of battering rams.

For many days Al Mamoun's men continued the slow, laborious task. After tunneling over 100 feet into the dark solid core, lighted only by flares, the men were discouraged to the point of despair. The flares consumed the oxygen in the narrow cavern and the men were becoming ill.

Then, as they pounded the limestone with their battering rams, they heard the muffled sound of something falling. The sound had come from the east of their bore. With renewed vigor they now worked excitedly toward the direction of the sound. Soon they broke into a hollow passage way. It was dark and frightening because of its low ceiling and the steep angle of its descent. On the floor before them lay a large angular stone that had been dislodged from the ceiling.

Photo courtesy Todd Alexander, Pyramid Productions, Inc.

Al Mamoun's forced entrance.

It was necessary to kneel on all fours to ascend the steep passage, but at the top they found the long lost secret entrance. It was found to be about 49 feet above the base of the Pyramid and about 24 feet east, or to the left, of the axis of the north face.

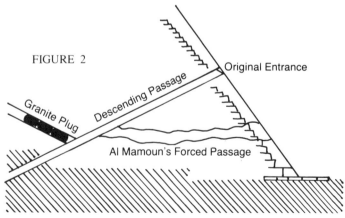

FIGURE 2

Original Entrance

Granite Plug

Descending Passage

Al Mamoun's Forced Passage

They then attempted the steep descent into the blackness below. It was a treacherous descent, and the lack of oxygen increased the danger of their mission. The passage was only about 3½ feet wide by a little less than 4 feet high, and sloped into the blackness below at an angle of slightly more than 26°.

After the perils of the treacherous descent, they were disappointed to find a roughly hewn chamber, empty except for dust and debris.

Returning on all fours, dusty and discouraged, they began the long upward climb. When they reached the large angular stone that had fallen from the ceiling they instinctively looked up. There above them was what seemed to be the beginning of a smoothly hewn passage, but completely filled by a tight-fitting mass of red and black granite.

The granite plug can now be seen in the ceiling of the Descending Passage. It was apparently placed there by the builders to prevent entrance to the passages and chambers above. Because these upper passages and chambers were unknown until A.D. 820, all other pyramids in Egypt, which are copies of the Great Pyramid, have only descending passages.

FIGURE 3

Al Mamoun's studies of the Great Pyramid had found no mention of any upward passages. Could this angular stone which fell have revealed a secret that had been hidden since the time of the Pyramid's construction?

The Queen's Chamber, showing the entrance to the low horizontal passage on the left, and the Niche in its east wall.

FIGURE 4

The thrill and excitement of discovery filled the men as they chipped away at the mass of granite that blocked the passage. But there was no way to dislodge it or to shatter it. The anticipation of what perhaps may lie ahead spurred them to attempt a bore around this huge block of granite to find a possible passage above it that would lead upward. They bored six feet into the limestone, only to find that the end of the granite plug was immediately followed by another granite plug, as tightly wedged as the first. Tunneling around the second granite plug they were only to find a third. They tunneled more than 16 feet. Beyond this was a limestone plug which was soft enough to remove by chiseling.

Finally they emerged into a steeply ascending passage. Again they must go on all fours, holding their torches low. They climbed this steep upward passage about 150 feet and suddenly emerged into a large opening where they could stand upright.

In the flickering light of their torches they could see another low ceilinged passage—this time a horizontal one.

Carefully making their way along this passage they came to a room approximately 18 feet long and nearly square, with a gabled roof. Discouraged at finding the room completely empty, they laboriously retraced their steps.

At the end of the passage they became aware of a large dark void above them. Raising their torches high, they found the precipitous edge of the floor of this dark upper passage. They found it was the same steep slippery slope as the other passages, but this time there were narrow ramps on either side with grooves for hand holds; and the ceiling was high enough to allow room in which to stand. The ceiling, in fact, disappeared into the darkness above. With renewed excitement Al Mamoun and his men ascended the steep passage, to find at its top another low horizontal passage. This led them into a small chamber where they could again stand. Beyond lay yet another low dark passage barely over 3 feet high through which they passed.

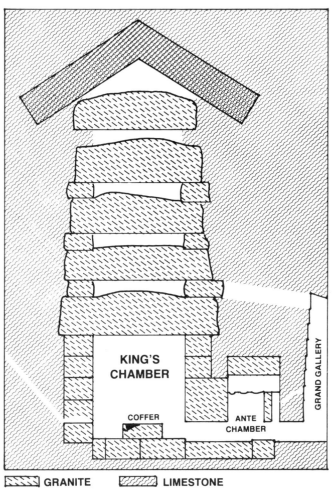

KING'S
CHAMBER

GRAND GALLERY

COFFER

ANTE
CHAMBER

GRANITE   LIMESTONE

FIGURE 5

Finally they emerged into a large room; the walls, floor and ceiling were of beautifully polished red granite. Because of its flat ceiling the men named it the King's Chamber.

Again the room was empty, containing only a lidless and empty granite box. The men were puzzled. Why did the box, that looked suspiciously like a sarcophagus, have no lid, and why did it contain no mummy? They reasoned, from their own difficulty in circumventing the three massive granite plugs that blocked and sealed the lower passageway, that it had been sealed by the builders and that no man had ever entered the upper chambers since. So why did it not contain a mummy? And if the lid had been removed, why could it not be found within the chamber, for surely it would have been too large to fit through the narrow passageways.

Al Mamoun came to the obvious conclusion that the chamber had been build *around* the granite box and that perhaps it had never contained either mummy or lid.

The celestial charts which he had hoped to find did not, in fact, exist. He found neither gold, nor treasure of any kind. The months of laborious effort proved to be an empty dream.

A few hieroglyphs were found in the chambers above the King's Chamber; one of the ovals was found to belong to King Khufu, and the others were apparently only quarry marks. All of the inscriptions were roughly drawn with red or black paint.

11

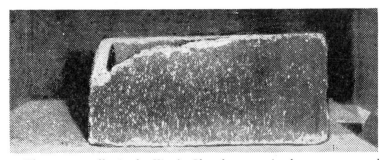

The empty coffer in the King's Chamber contained no mummy, and a lid has never been found.

In succeeding centuries the Arabs stripped the Pyramid of many of its beautiful white casing stones to build the new capital city of El Kaherah. Later the remainder of them were removed and dragged to Cairo to build their mosques and palaces. The "Jewel in the Desert" had been violated like a lovely virgin.

Fortunately for us the marauders left unnoticed a few of the casing stones which lay beneath the rubble at its base.

In 1836 Colonel Howard-Vyse undertook the tumultous task of clearing away the rubble of limestone, sand and debris that had accumulated through the centuries. It was a foreboding task, as some of the piles were as much as fifty feet high. He decided first to clear away a pile from the center of the north side to see if he could get down to the very base of the Pyramid. To his complete delight he found the few original polished limestone casing stones still intact and in the spot where the builders had placed them.

This discovery not only silenced forever the age-old debate concerning the fact-or-fiction of the existence of such stones, but it enabled us to determine accurately the original angle of the sides from base to apex, and thus its true proportions.

These casing stones were so finely carved and polished and, in the words of Howard-Vyse, "...in a sloping plane as correct and true almost as modern work by optical instrument makers.

The joints were scarcely perceptible, not wider than the thickness of silver paper.'' He found the angle to be 51° 51' 14.3".

The magnitude of this discovery is tremendous. It has opened fo. us a world of knowledge and insight into the origin and purpose of the Great Pyramid and into the astounding knowledge and understanding of its builders; and we are faced with the realization that ancient man, our forefathers 4,000 years removed, were not the ignorant barbarians that we have been taught to believe. They were intelligent men, with a knowledge of the universe in which they lived.

Science and astronomy today can give us the size relationship of the earth and its moon. Did man, 4,000 years ago, know this relationship? If we were to place the circle of the moon tangent to the circle of the earth (as in Figure 6), the exact proportions of the Great Pyramid can be constructed on their combined radii, showing the casing stone angle of 51° 51'. Did the builders of the Pyramid know the size of the earth and its moon? How could they?

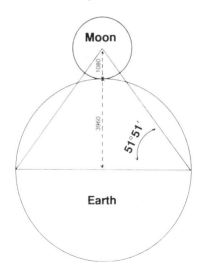

FIGURE 6

13

THE MAGNIFICENT NUMBERS

The magnificent numbers found in the geometry of the Great Pyramid reveal a wisdom and understanding far beyond the possibilities of man. Who then was the architect?

Nearly all of the Great Pyramid's beautiful white casing stones have been stripped from its sides to build the capital city of El Kaherah. In 1836 Colonel Howard-Vyse discovered a few of these casing stones under tons of rock and rubble at the base of the north face. Their enormity is shown by the size relationship to the man standing beside them.

2

Stonehenge— another Wonder!

When Colonel Howard-Vyse unearthed the casing stones from the tons of rubble and debris, he in fact unearthed a great secret, worth far more than the treasures that Caliph Al Mamoun had hoped to find.

Al Mamoun had found no celestial maps, no gold nor precious stones, not even any hieroglyphs. The only thing he found was rubble, dust and centuries of bat dung.

The discovery of the casing stones, however, was a virtual gold mine. It now enabled archaeologists to find the long-sought original height of the Pyramid—484.90 feet (or roughly 485 feet) from its mean socket level to the top of its beautiful gold topstone.[1]

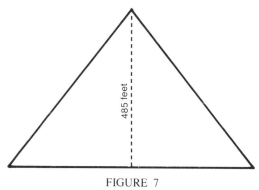

485 feet

FIGURE 7

---

[1] A theoretical height, for the topstone was apparently never placed.

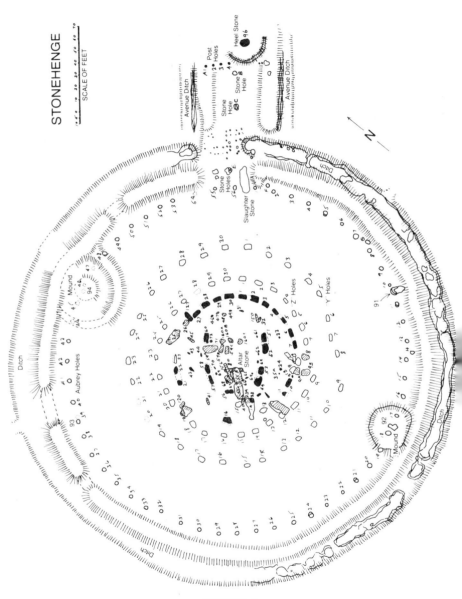

FIGURE 8

16

STONEHENGE—ANOTHER WONDER!

The angle of the casing stones, now known as the Pyramid angle—51° 51′ 14.3″—was discovered to be the π angle, giving to the vertical height the same ratio to its square base as the radius of a circle bears to its circumference.

It would cause us to wonder about the mathematical knowledge of man 4,000 years ago. Either they knew the π relationship, or the architect was perhaps not a man!

As remarkable as the discovery of π may be, there is yet a further and more astounding relationship involving this magnificent number.

On the lonely wind-swept Salisbury Plain in the southern part of England stands another ancient stone monument, Stonehenge.[2] A 4,000 year old mystery still shrouds those cold and lonely stones like the mists that hang heavily over the plain.

In all the ages since its construction, men have built nothing comparable to Stonehenge. Like the Great Pyramid, the solutions to the mystery that surrounds its construction, its architect and its purpose have been sincerely sought by scientists, theologians, archaeologists and historians. But, like the Great Pyramid, Stonehenge has now begun to give up its secrets.

Stonehenge consists of several concentric circles, with two inner circles spread at the ends to form U-shaped arrangements called "horseshoes." Beyond these circles, standing all alone is a large natural monolith called the Heel Stone.

The inmost arrangement of stones is called the Bluestone Horseshoe, because of their blueish-green color when wet. Outside the arrangement of bluestones, and dwarfing them by their enormity, stand the stones of the Trilithon Horseshoe. These are free-standing units consisting of two uprights topped by a lintel. There are five of these trilithons. They are of *sarsen,* a kind of natural sandstone. They form a set of frames through which the sunrise, sunset, moonrise and moonset can

---

[2] For a full description of the origin and purpose of Stonehenge: Bonnie Gaunt, *Stonehenge...a closer look,* Bell Books, Crown Publishing Co., New York, 1982.

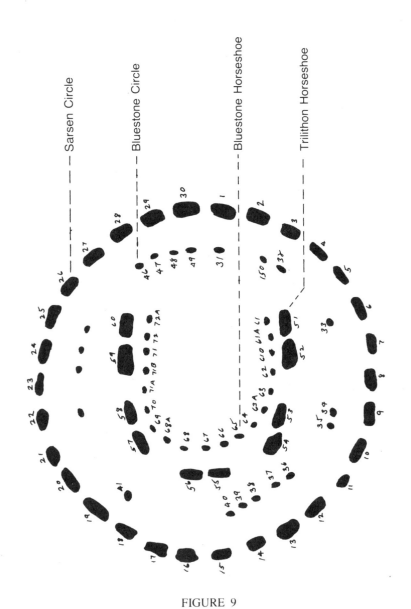

FIGURE 9

STONEHENGE—ANOTHER WONDER!

Artist's conception of Stonehenge at the time of its completion. This illustration shows more stones in the Bluestone Circle than probably actually existed.

be viewed at the equinoxes and solstices. Both the Bluestone and Trilithon Horseshoes are open to the northeast, in the direction of summer sunrise.

Surrounding the trilithons is the Bluestone Circle. Only 20 of the original stones of this circle can be seen above ground today.

Immediately outside the Bluestone Circle is the Sarsen Circle. It was originally composed of 30 uprights topped by 30 lintels. They are of sarsen from whence it derives its name. The inner faces of these uprights were dressed and polished.

Far out beyond the Sarsen Circle lies the Aubrey Circle. This is a circle of small holes, so named for their discoverer, John Aubrey, who found them in 1666. There are 56 holes in the circle, 32 of which have been covered by cement markers for purposes of observation for tourists.

Standing approximately on the line of the Aubrey Circle are the four Station Stones. They formed a rectangle perpendicular to the summer sunrise. Only two of these stones remain today, and one of them is lying on its face.

Photo by Thomas Gilbert

The one remaining stone of the great Central Trilithon dwarfs Bluestone No. 68. This giant sarsen is the largest hand worked stone in Britain, weighing 50 tons.

Surrounding the Aubrey Circle is a bank and ditch. This bank is thought to have been about 6 feet high and about 20 feet wide, forming an outer barrier or wall of the monument. The bank was composed of white chalk, which makes up most of the surface of the region around Stonehenge. It is supposed that this bank, as well as acting as a barrier for the enclosure, also served as a horizon for the viewing of the sun and moon through the stone archways. There was a 35-foot opening in the bank at the entrance, facing the summer sunrise.

To the northeast of the circle stands the Heel Stone. It stands alone and separate from the monument, yet is a vital part of its function, for it served as a marker for the sunrise at the summer solstice. It has long been called the Sunstone. The name Heel Stone was probably derived from the Greek *helios,* which is sun. Some claim it came from the Welsh word for sun, *haul,* (pronounced ''hayil''). Regardless of its origin, it is definitely the sun stone, for it stands outside the entrance, marking the northernmost extreme of the summer sun at the solstice.

Some have suggested that the Heel Stone was the most important stone of the monument. This would be comparable to saying that the hands are the most important part of a clock. They are important indeed, but would point to nothing of value unless the remaining parts of the clock were functioning according to design.

The Heel Stone does indeed tell the time at Stonehenge. Since its construction 4,000 years ago, to the observer who stands in the center of the Sarsen Circle, the sun appears to rest atop the Heel Stone on the morning of summer solstice.[3]

Professor Wm. Flinders Petrie, commenting on this, wrote in 1880: ''The large numbers of people that keep up with much energy the custom of seeing the sun rise at midsummer, somewhat suggests that it is an old tradition; and hence that it has

---

[3] The precession of the equinoxes has not separated the sun from its appearance atop the Heel Stone. A description of this phenomenon is given in Appendix I, which please see.

The famous Heel Stone or Sunstone. Some say its name is derived from the Greek "helios," meaning "sun."

some weight, independent of the mere coincidence.''[4]

It was no ''mere coincidence'' that the summer sun rises over the Heel Stone. It was planned precision.

And what beautiful, magnificent precision! The azimuth of that sunrise is 51° 51' 14.3" from north. The word ''coincidence'' has no place here. The architect of Stonehenge has preserved in stone for all the remaining generations of man, even to this day, the precise Pyramid angle!

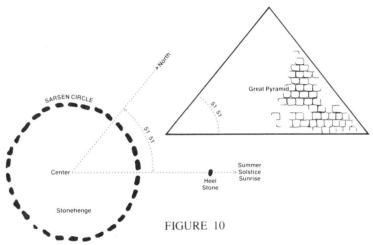

FIGURE 10

This astounding fact raises some profound questions. How did the builder of Stonehenge know the Pyramid angle? Or did he? How did the builder of the Great Pyramid know the angle of sunrise to north on the far away and desolate island we now call England? The alignment of summer solstice sunrise, as Professor Gerald Hawkins has so succinctly stated, ''is not man-maneuverable,'' and, it might be added, neither is the direction of north.

The next obvious question is, of course, what has Stonehenge to do with the Great Pyramid? Was the one known to the

---

[4] Wm. Flinders Petrie, *Stonehenge, Plans, Description, and Theories,* Edward Stanford, London, 1880, p. 20.

builder of the other? Did they share a common architect? What man, 4,000 years ago, could possibly have known such relationships as the diameter of the earth, or the radius of our moon, or the azimuth of sunrise in a precise spot in a land 2,300 miles away? Or was it a man?

The architect of Stonehenge did not leave us without some answers.

On the circumference of the Aubrey Circle, the outer circle of 56 holes, there were four Station Stones which were so placed as to form a rectangle which was perpendicular to the summer solstice sunrise. Only two of those stones remain today. If we were to start walking from Station Stone 93 to Station Stone 91, and keep walking in that same direction, we would eventually bump into the Great Pyramid. In other words, the exact azimuth from Station Stone 93 to Station Stone 91 is, in fact, the arc of a great circle that passes through both

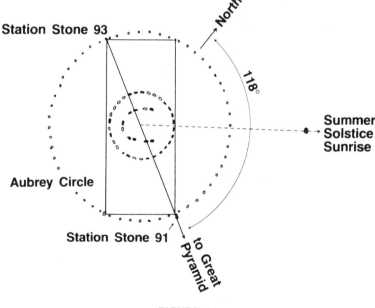

FIGURE 11

Stonehenge and the Great Pyramid.[6] The architect of Stonehenge has left for us a road map, if you please, pointing directly toward the Great Pyramid. The diagonal of the Station Stone rectangle becomes just such a pointer.

The rectangular placement of the Station Stones at Stonehenge was important because they served as sun and moon alignments. Stones 92-91 (the short side of the rectangle) parallel the Stonehenge axis, which is the solstice line; hence this alignment points to the sunrise at the summer solstice. At the same time, the long sides of the rectangle are aligned with the moonrise *low* nearest the solstice. The diagonal (from stone 93 to stone 91, which points to the Pyramid) is aligned with the moonrise *high* nearest the summer solstice.

If we were to attempt to move Stonehenge a few miles north or a few miles south, the Station Stones would have to form a parallelogram to align with the sun and moon, and it would no longer point directly toward the Great Pyramid. Stonehenge is at latitude north 51.17°, and at this latitude the solstice movements of the sun and moon form a rectangle. How did the architect know the only latitude in the northern hemisphere that would make this unique geometry possible?

The diagonal of the Station Stone rectangle is an arc of a great circle which passes through both Stonehenge and the Great Pyramid. It not only points directly to the Pyramid, it also points toward the summer moonrise at the high point of its swing. If this great circle were divided by the unit known as the Pyramid geographical mile,[7] it would divide an even 21,600 times, or as many times as there are "minutes" in the complete circle (one minute of arc would be one Pyramid geographical mile).[8]

The number 21,600 becomes one of the magnificent num-

---

[6] This angle can be obtained by using a globe, or it can be computed by spherical trigonometry.

[7] The Pyramid geographical mile (6,082 feet), is twice the rock level perimeter. If based on the earth diameter of 7,920 miles, 1/21600 of the great circle of earth would be 6,082 feet.

bers of the Great Pyramid and Stonehenge, for the arc of this great circle is pointing both to the moon and to the Pyramid, and the lunar number is 2160 (the number of miles in its diameter).

How did the builder of Stonehenge know anything about great circles? A yet more profound question raises its head: did the builders of the Great Pyramid and of Stonehenge know the diameter of the moon? Was this the plan of some great architect, or was it a coincidence of mathematics?

An encounter with such an unlikely coincidence causes us to take another look at the Station Stone rectangle. How could it have been so strategically placed on the face of our globe to reveal such precision? Yet, it was merely four rough, unhewn stones—sublime magnificence and absurd simplicity! We stand in awe, yes, even reverence; for true science is not so much the solving of problems as it is an encounter with mysteries which are less to be solved than they are to be revered.

This simple rectangle, marked by four rough stones, bears another number which is common to both Stonehenge and the Great Pyramid. It is the number 288. The diagonal of the Station Stone rectangle which forms the arc of the great circle, measures 288 feet. Since these Station Stones stand in the line of the Aubrey Circle, it means that this diagonal is the same length as the diameter of the circle, for they share a common center point. This Aubrey Circle was the outermost circle of the monument (the bank and ditch forming the barrier beyond), thus it could be thought of as performing a similar function in relation to the monument as the square base of the Great Pyramid relates to its structure within.

The four corners of the Pyramid rest upon sockets that were sunk into the natural rock to an average depth of 9+ inches.[9] Is

---

[8] Morton Edgar, *The Great Pyramid,* Maclure, Macdonald & Co., 1924, p. 194.

[9] Each side of the Pyramid at the rock base level measures 760⅓+ feet, making the perimeter 3041+ feet. The reed is 10.56 feet, thus: 3041 ÷ 10.56 = 288.

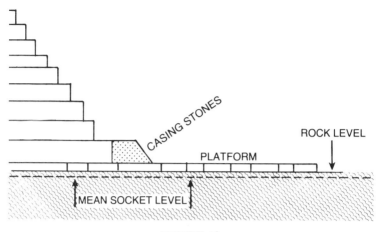

ROCK LEVEL

CASING STONES

PLATFORM

MEAN SOCKET LEVEL

FIGURE 12

it coincidence that the perimeter of the Pyramid at this rock base level measures 288 in another ancient unit, the reed?[10] This unit first appeared in historical records in ancient Jewish manuscripts, when the prophet Ezekiel recorded a vision in which he saw a beautiful temple. He was told, in vision, to measure the temple with an instrument called a *reed*. Research has found this unit to be 10.56 feet.

The outer circumference of Stonehenge, *i.e.*, the Aubrey Circle, is therefore found to bear the same number as the perimeter of the Great Pyramid. And what a beautiful number it turns out to be! A magnificent number indeed.

If the diameter of the Aubrey Circle measures 288 feet, the radius would be 144 feet. The perimeter of the Station Stone rectangle is .144 of a mile while each side of the Great Pyramid at its rock base level measures .144 of a mile. If the circumference of the inner face of the Sarsen Circle at Stonehenge were re-defined as the perimeter of a square, one side of that square would be 144 royal cubits. Why 144? Aside from its being the result of 12 × 12, what does the number mean?

---

[10] The length of the reed will be further explained in Chapter 3.

THE MAGNIFICENT NUMBERS

In the year A.D. 90, John, the Apostle of Jesus, had a vision while in exile on the Isle of Patmos in the Mediterranean. In the vision he saw 144 thousand saints standing with the Lamb of God on Mount Zion. It was a glorious vision in which he experienced a glimpse of the wonder and the beauty of heaven.

What has the Bible to do with the Great Pyramid, or with Stonehenge? Could it be possible that the Bible holds a clue to the solving of the mysteries surrounding these two ancient monuments?

Why have those two stone structures come down to us from what seems to have been "time immemorial?" Why have they endured the ravages of time and tempest, and the vandalism of man? Are there great truths yet to be found? Thomas Huxley once wrote, "Time, whose tooth gnaws away everything else, is powerless against truth." If the Great Pyramid and Stonehenge hide the truths of past ages, then the quest for such truth is a noble pursuit, for time is indeed powerless against truth.

Jeremy Collier once said, "We must not let go manifest truths because we cannot answer all questions about them." Truth! Elusive friend! Many are the truths already unearthed and discovered at Stonehenge and the Pyramid. Those truths that have been found are not to be discarded simply because we cannot answer all the questions about them. Emerson said "The greatest homage we can pay to truth is to use it." Surely, that which is seen, must not be sacrificed to that which is not seen. There are many questions regarding these two magnificent monuments for which previous generations have given us no answers, but the pursuit of those answers remains a "glorious quest."

28

3

The Wonderful Numberer

In the year 547 B.C., Daniel, a Hebrew captive in Babylon, saw a vision which carried him into the vast unknown future. At the conclusion of the vision he saw what appeared to be an angel speak to another angel and ask concerning the time when the vision would be fulfilled. The second heavenly personage was called, in Hebrew, *Palmoni* פלמוני , The Wonderful Numberer, or The Numberer of Secrets. We are given no description of this Wonderful Numberer, and he is never mentioned again by this name in the Hebrew scriptures.

The Numberer of Secrets, *Palmoni,* is an interesting title. Surely the secrets that have been locked up in numbers have touched the lives of men for thousands of years.

The Hebrews used a numbering system based on the letters of their alphabet, each letter bearing a number. Thus every word in Hebrew also has a numeric value, often revealing a hidden meaning. The Wonderful Number, *Palmoni,* bears the number 216, which is the lunar number (2160). This ancient system of numbering is known as gematria.

Each side 216 — Diameter of Moon 2,160 miles
Perimeter 864 — Diameter of Sun 864,000 miles

THE MAGNIFICENT NUMBERS

Pythagoras seems to have discovered a great truth when he said, "Numbers are the language of the universe." They do indeed appear to be the building blocks of creation and the key to unlock the mysteries of the origin and destiny of man. The magnificent numbers of the Great Pyramid and Stonehenge have a startling correlation with these numbers which have to do with man's destiny. The key unlocks a beautiful and majestic plan that touches the lives of every one of us.

The Apostle John so beautifully and succinctly capsulized the vast work of creation in the first chapter of his Gospel by telling us that Jesus, in his pre-human condition as a glorious being called the Logos, or Word, created all things. He said, *"All things were made by him, and without him was not anything made that was made."*

The very foundation of all creation is built upon the number 12. The word "creation" in the language of the New Testament, Greek, is κτισις, which has a number value of 740. The simple equation, $12 \times 74 = 888$, becomes alive with meaning when we realize that the name Jesus in Greek, 'Ιησους, has a number value of 888. And how appropriate it is to find that $12 + 74 = 86$, for it is the number of God (*Elohim* אלהים, 86). *"In the beginning God (Elohim) created the heavens and the earth."* (Genesis 1:1)

The two languages of the Bible both incorporated the numbering system we know as gematria. The discovery of these number codes is not new. The noted Bible expositor, E. W. Bullinger, was among many who have added to our understanding of this vast subject. His book *Number in Scripture*, first published in 1894, shows the supernatural design in the use of numbers, both in the works of God and in the word of God. Another expositor, Ivan Panin, published his "Bible Numerics" articles in 1912. More recently published is the exciting work of Jerry Lucas and Del Washburn, *Theomatics* (Stein and Day, New York, 1977). These two dedicated students, using a Greek Interlinear New Testament, translated every word from the Greek to its number equivalent. Their startling analogies are enough to convince even the most determined skeptic. They called it ''God's best kept secret.''

Hebrew, the language of the Old Testament, has twenty two letters in its alphabet. Their number equivalents are listed below:

Letter	Name	Number
א	'Aleph	1
ב	Bêyth	2
ג	Giymel	3
ד	Dâleth	4
ה	Hê'	5
ו	Vâv	6
ז	Zayin	7
ח	Chêyth	8
ט	Têyth	9
י	Yôwd	10
כ, final ך	Kaph	20
ל	Lâmed	30
מ, final ם	Mêm	40
נ, final ן	Nûwn	50
ס	Çâmek	60
ע	'Ayin	70
{ פ, final ף	Phê'	80
{ פ	Pê'	
צ, final ץ	Tsâdêy	90
ק	Qôwph	100
ר	Rêysh	200
{ שׂ	Sîyn	300
{ שׁ	Shîyn	
{ ת	Thâv	400
{ ת	Tâv	

THE MAGNIFICENT NUMBERS

The Greek alphabet uses twenty six letters, two of which have become extinct. Their number values appear below:

α	. . . .	.Alpha	1
β б	. . . .	.Beta	2
γ	. . . .	.Gamma	3
δ	. . . .	.Delta	4
ε	. . . .	.Epsilon	5
ζ	. . . .	.Zeta	7
η	. . . .	.Eta	8
θ ϑ	. . . .	.Theta	9
ι	. . . .	.Iota	10
κ	. . . .	.Kappa	20
λ	. . . .	.Lambda	30
μ	. . . .	.Mu	40
ν	. . . .	.Nu	50
ξ	. . . .	.Xi	60
ο	. . . .	.Omicron	70
π	. . . .	.Pi	80
ρ	. . . .	.Rho	100
σ	final ς	.Sigma	200
τ	. . . .	.Tau	300
υ	. . . .	.Upsilon	400
φ ϕ	. . . .	.Phi	500
χ	. . . .	.Chi	600
ψ	. . . .	.Psi	700
ω	. . . .	.Omega	800

THE WONDERFUL NUMBERER

To give an example of how gematria is used, let's take the best known name in the New Testament—Lord Jesus Christ:

κ	= 20	ι	= 10	Χ	= 600
υ	= 400	η	= 8	ρ	= 100
ρ	= 100	σ	= 200	ι	= 10
ι	= 10	ο	= 70	σ	= 200
ο	= 70	υ	= 400	τ	= 300
ς	= 200	ς	= 200	ο	= 70
	800		888	ς	= 200
					1480

Lord (800) Jesus (888) Christ (1480) = 3168

Why do the magnificent numbers of the Great Pyramid and Stonehenge correlate with the gematria of the Bible and the geometry of the earth, sun and moon? What great plan of the Creator has been kept secret through the centuries, locked in number, locked in stone?

What does the Great Pyramid have to do with the Bible? Is it even mentioned in the Bible? After all, the Pyramid was certainly in existence before most of the Bible was even written.

The prophet Isaiah wrote of a monument in Egypt that would serve as a witness. The scripture reads:

In that day shall there be an altar to the Lord in the midst of the land of Egypt, and a pillar at the border thereof to the Lord. And it shall be for a sign, and for a witness unto the Lord of Hosts in the land of Egypt. (Isaiah 19:19-20)

Isaiah has defined the exact geographical position of this altar-monument: *"In the midst of the land of Egypt"* and yet *"at the border thereof."* There is only one spot on the face of the earth that answers to this description, and on that precise spot, the Great Pyramid stands. But how can it be in the *midst* and yet at the *border*? This apparent contradiction in terms is, in fact, an accurate and concise description of the position of

33

the Pyramid in relation to the unique shape of the land of Egypt.

This remarkable position of the Pyramid was first noticed in 1868 by Henry Mitchell, Chief Hydrographer of the United States Coastal Survey. He found that the regularity of the general curvature of the coast of the Nile Delta forms a quadrant. This led him to wonder what point marked the center of that quadrant. To his astonishment he found the Great Pyramid sitting on the precise spot. With this discovery he exclaimed, "That monument stands in a more important physical situation than any other building erected by man."

Commenting on Mitchell's discovery, Professor C. Piazzi Smyth, Astronomer Royal for Scotland, said:

Now Lower Egypt being as already described, of a sector, still more exactly than of a Delta shape, it must have its centre, not like a circle in the middle of its surface, but at one extreme corner thereof. Whereupon Mr. Mitchell has acutely remarked that the building which stands at, or just raised above, such a *sectorial* centre must be at one and the same time both at the border thereof, and yet at its *quasi,* or practically governing, middle. That is to say, just as was to be that grandly honored prophetic monument, pure and undefiled in its religious bearing, though in an idolatrous Egyptian land, alluded to by Isaiah (Chapter 19); for was it not fore-ordained by the Divine Word to be both *"an altar to the Lord in the midst of the land of Egypt, and a pillar at the border thereof"*—an apparent mechanical impossibility, yet realised in the sectorial centre condition of the Great Pyramid.

Aside from its geometrical and geographical relationship to Isaiah's prophecy, when we assign the numerical equivalents to each of the Hebrew words in the text we become aware of an amazing mathematical relationship. As shown in the table below, Isaiah 19:19-20 adds up to 5,449. The actual height of the Great Pyramid to its summit platform as the builders left it

Height of the Great Pyramid in
Pyramid inches, to the original
summit platform 5,449

was 5,449 Pyramid inches.[1] All the numerical values of the Hebrew text are shown in the table below. This remarkable numerical identity of Isaiah 19:19-20 was discovered by O. de Blaere, of Antwerp, Belgium.

The Great Pyramid has come to be known as the only remaining one of the Ancient Wonders of the World. How fitting that it should be called by this name, for it truly is a wonder of all wonders. We have seen from the foregoing demonstration of the gematria of Isaiah 19:19-20 the Scriptural identification of the Pyramid. There is yet another mention of this ancient wonder by one of the Hebrew prophets—Jeremiah.

"The Great, the Mighty God, the Lord of Hosts is his name... which hast set signs and wonders in the land of Egypt, even to this day, and in Israel, and among other men." (Jeremiah 32:18-20)

The word *wonders* in this verse is the Hebrew word ומפתים, and by gematria it bears the number 576. It is clearly an identification of both the Great Pyramid and Stonehenge. We have seen the remarkable correlation of the outer circle of Stonehenge, the Aubrey Circle, with the base perimeter of the Pyramid. The diameter of the Aubrey Circle is 288 feet, and the rock base perimeter of the Pyramid is 288 reeds. Both monuments bear this magnificent number, for they are both *wonders* — 2 × 288 = 576!

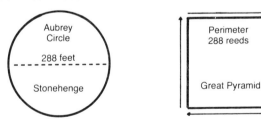

FIGURE 13

[1] The Pyramid inch was a unit of measure in the structural design of the Great Pyramid. It is described as 1 Pyramid inch equals 1.00106 British inches or 1 British inch equals .99894 of a Pyramid inch.

A square with sides of 288 has a perimeter of 1152, and the number 1152 is found to be the gematria for *witness* μαρτυριας. Isaiah prophesied that the Great Pyramid would be for a sign and a *witness*.

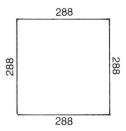

Each side, 288— Pyramid base perimeter, 288 reeds
Perimeter, 1152—Witness, μαρτυριας 1152

In the year 1865 Professor C. Piazzi Smyth took measurements of the Great Pyramid. On the basis of those measurements he was able to extrapolate the fact that π (3.14159) and y (365.242) constitute the basis of the Pyramid's geometric construction; the value of y being the number of days in the solar tropical year. At the time of this great undertaking, the base of the monument lay buried under huge piles of sand and debris, and an actual measurement was not possible. Therefore he computed the base perimeter on the constructural basis of π and y, and suggested that the base side length would be 365.242 sacred cubits, or the number of sacred cubits as there are days required for the earth to orbit the sun.

Many years later, after the rubble had been cleared away, modern surveys were undertaken and an accurate measurement could be obtained. The results were startling! They uncovered rectangular sockets beneath each of the four corners, and the survey showed that the original full design of the structure did indeed have a base side length of 365.242 sacred cubits, giving a total base perimeter of 36524.2 Pyramid inches.

William Petrie, father of Professor Wm. Flinders Petrie, was curious about this relationship of the base perimeter to the earth's orbit around the sun. He pictured the base of the structure as representing the orbit of earth, and the apex with its glorious topstone as representing the sun.[2] He reasoned that the distance from the earth to the sun could therefore be represented by its height. The measure from the mean socket level to the apex is 485 feet, and when it is converted into miles it becomes .091856 of a mile. When this figure is multiplied by 1000-million it becomes 91,856,000 miles, or approximately the distance from earth to the sun at its perihelion. Was the builder of that great monument showing us its relationship to the sun? Or was it just a mathematical coincidence?

In 1973 I began a study of the correlation of Stonehenge with the Great Pyramid. I had long been aware of this remarkable earth-sun indication in the height of the Pyramid, thus it was logical to ask: "Could Stonehenge also show earth's distance from the sun?" If it did, where would we look? What is there at Stonehenge that points to the sun?

Every year, on the morning of summer solstice, crowds gather at Stonehenge to watch the sunrise. It has become the tradition of centuries. To one standing in the center of the Sarsen Circle, the rising sun on the morning of summer solstice appears to be perched atop the Heel Stone. The whole orientation of the monument is built around this alignment. The Heel Stone was once called the Sunstone, for this reason. The circles of the monument, on the other hand, seem to pertain to the earth. Could the separation of the Heel Stone from the rest of the monument be telling us something?

Out of simple curiosity, I multiplied the distance from the Sarsen Center to the base of the Heel Stone (256 feet) by the number of days in the solar tropical year, and to my complete delight, found that the product times 1,000 is the mean distance from earth to the sun. (256 × 365.242 — 93,500.00) The

---

[2] The topstone of the Pyramid was used metaphorically of Jesus in I Peter 2:6. By gematria, topstone bears the number 864 γωνια, which is the solar number (864,000 miles = diameter of the sun).

mean distance from earth to the sun is about 93 million miles. Obviously, the placing of the Heel Stone at that precise distance was not by accident; it was engineered by one who knew the geometry of the universe!

Geometry is, of course, based upon units of measure. Through the centuries of man's history many units have been used. In the English speaking countries we have been conditioned to think of linear measure in terms of the mile, foot and inch; and now we are being re-educated to think in terms of the meter. What units did the ancients use? Was the mile unit known to them? Do we have evidence indicating the units used in the construction of the Great Pyramid, or of Stonehenge?

There has been considerable controversy over the linear unit used in the construction of the Pyramid. Some point to several different units having been used, but most all agree that the ancient Sacred Cubit is basic to its construction.

The Sacred Cubit is found to bear an exact relationship to the size of the earth, i.e., it is earth commensurate. This cubit is exactly one 10,000,000th of the mean polar radius of the earth, which the latest geodetic research reveals to be 3949.9 miles. If we divide this figure by 10,000,000 the result is 25.0266 British inches, the precise length of the Sacred Cubit. Thus the mean polar radius of the earth measures 250,000,000

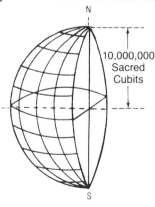

10,000,000
Sacred
Cubits

Pyramid inches.[3] The Pyramid inch equals 1.001064 British inches.

Another linear unit used in the construction of the Great Pyramid was the Royal Cubit. This is generally stated as 1.72 feet, or 20.64 inches. Precisely it has been defined as 1.7203907 feet. It is the best known of the ancient Egyptian measures and is derived from the diagonal of one square remen. The Egyptian remen was 1.2165 feet.

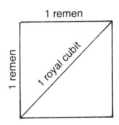

Another cubit, which is believed to be the unit used in the construction of Solomon's Temple in ancient Israel is the Sumerian cubit of 1.65 feet, or 19.8 inches.[4][5] This unit is of great antiquity and is found to relate to the diameter of the earth thus: 400 × 19.8 = 7920. The mean diameter of the earth is 7920 miles. This unit also bears a relationship to both Stonehenge and the Great Pyramid as will be demonstrated subsequently.

A. Thom, in his studies of Stonehenge, and other megalithic sites in Britain, found the use of yet another unit, *i.e.*, the megalithic yard, which is 2.72 feet, and its relative, the megalithic mile which is 2.727272 miles (or 14,400 feet). This

---

[3]Adam Rutherford, *Pyramidology Book I*, The Institute of Pyramidology, Hertfordshire, Great Britain, 1970, p. 75.

[4]Encyclopedia Judaica, Keter Publishing House, Jerusalem, 1972, p.947

[5] A. E. Berriman, *Historical Metrology*, J. M. Dent & Sons, LTD, London, 1953, p. 29.

unit—2.72 feet—was observed by John Michell[6] to be identical to an ancient unit which is still in use in the far East, called the *pu*. It is called the megalithic mile (MMi) because its ratio to the British mile is virtually the same as the megalithic yard is to the British foot. The cosmological relationship between the megalithic mile and the British mile is remarkable:

Diameter of the earth ....7920 British miles

Diameter of the moon ....792 MMi

Perimeter of a square containing
    the circle of the earth ....31,680 British miles

Perimeter of a square containing
    the circle of the moon ....3,168 MMi

Diameter of the sun ....316,800 MMi

(Mean circumference of the Sarsen Circle .....316.8 feet)

In the year 573 B.C. the Hebrew prophet, Ezekiel, recorded a vision in which he saw a beautiful temple and city. In the vision he was given the unit of measure upon which they were to be constructed.

> *"...and in the man's hand a measuring reed of six great cubits long, by the cubit and a hand breadth..." "The cubit is a cubit and a hand breadth..."* (Ezekiel 40:5; 43:13)

What was meant by the great cubit? What was its measure? Herodotus, the "father of history," mentioned the use of the royal cubit in Babylon at that time, and a shorter one called the moderate cubit. In the Mishna the moderate cubit is defined as six hand breadths or 144 barleycorns. This moderate cubit is generally accepted by historians and archaeologists as 18.14 inches, thus a hand breadth would be 3.02 inches. But the reed of six great cubits with which the temple and city were measured is defined as using a cubit which was called a *"cubit and a hand breadth."* The moderate cubit of 18.14 inches, with the addition of one more hand breadth would become 1.76 feet. How

---

[6]John Michell, *City of Revelation*, Ballantine Books, New York, p. 119.

41

remarkable to find that our British mile which is in use today measures an even 3,000 great cubits.

The reed was to be six great cubits in length, thus $6 \times 1.76 = 10.56$ feet. The relationship of this unit to Stonehenge becomes apparent when we remember that each of the lintels which topped the Sarsen Circle had a mean length of 10.56 feet—the length of one reed. But the relationship becomes even more startling when we find that all of the Stonehenge circles, with the exception of the Aubrey Circle, are evenly divisible by the great cubit. Was this unit used by the builder? The great cubit was not recorded in history until 573 B.C., yet it was apparently known to the builder of Stonehenge 1,400 years before Ezekiel saw the vision.

	Feet	Great Cubits	Reeds
Circumference of mean of Sarsen Circle ..	316.8	180	30
Diameter of outer face of Sarsen Circle ...	105.6	60	10
Diameter of Bluestone Circle	79.2	45	22½
Circumference of outer face of Inner Bank	1056	600	100
Each Lintel	10.56	6	1
Interval between Sarsen uprights	3.52	2	⅓
Long side of Station Stone Rectangle	264	150	25
Diameter of Bluestone Horseshoe	39.6	22½	

The great cubit and the reed bear a remarkable relationship to the Great Pyramid, for the perimeter at the rock base level measures 288 reeds. It is also commensurate with the geometry of the universe as shown below. The dimensions of the earth, sun and moon are evenly divisible by this unit, evidencing that the Creator of these orbs used this unit.

Diameter	Miles	Feet	Great Cubits	Reeds
of sun ..	864,000	4,561,920,000	2,592,000,000	432,000,000
Diameter of earth ..	7,920	41,817,600	23,760,000	3,960,000
Diameter of moon..	2,160	11,404,800	6,480,000	1,080,000

The reed bears an interesting relationship to the British mile, thus:

Diameter of sun ....432,000,000 reeds
Radius of sun ....432,000 miles
Diameter of earth...........................3,960,000 reeds
Radius of earth ....3,960 miles
Diameter of moon ....1,080,000 reeds
Radius of moon................................1,080 miles

The great cubit and the reed also bear a relationship to Jesus by the gematria of his name.

$8 \times 1.76 = 14.08$ ....Saviour, $\sigma\omega\tau\eta\rho$, 1408
$13 \times 1.76 = 22.88$ ...Christ the Lord, $X\rho\iota\sigma\tau\sigma\varsigma$ $K\upsilon\rho\iota\sigma\varsigma$, 2288
$3 \times 10.56 = 31.68$ ...Lord Jesus Christ,
                      $K\upsilon\rho\iota\sigma\varsigma$ $'I\eta\sigma\sigma\upsilon\varsigma$ $X\rho\iota\sigma\tau\sigma\varsigma$, 3168
$2 \times 10.56 = 2112$ ...."*A virgin shall conceive and bear a son, and*
                      shall call his name Immanuel.'' (Isaiah7:14)
                      , העלמה הרה וילדת בן וקראת שמו עמנו אל
                      2112

1056 = *The joy of thy salvation* (Psalm 51:12) ששון ישעך

The mile unit is found to be interrelated to the other units of ancient metrology, and as the harmony of the mile with the universe continues to unfold in this and subsequent chapters, it will become self-evident that its origins were not the arbitrary work of man, but were a part of the numbering system involved in creation. The antiquity of this unit is evident from its relation to the Great Pyramid and Stonehenge. If it were a unit devised by man, the interrelationships which we observe would not be possible.

When the dimensions of the earth, sun and moon are stated in terms of the mile unit, the numbers harmonize with the geometry and gematria of the Bible, with the divisions of time, and with the magnificent numbers of the Great Pyramid and Stonehenge.

Diameter of sun = 864,000 British miles
  86,400 = Seconds in one day
  8,640 = Acres in six sides of the New Jerusalem (Rev. 21:16)
  864 = Great cubits in two sides of the Great Pyramid (rock level)

Diameter of earth = 7,920 British miles
  7,920 = Minutes in eleven half days
  79.2 = Feet in diameter of Bluestone Circle (Stonehenge)
  $792 \times 4 = 3168$, Lord Jesus Christ

Diameter of moon = 2,160 British miles
  2,160 = Minutes in three half days
  216 = Palmoni פלמוני, The Wonderful Numberer
  $216 \times 4 = 864$, Corner Stone $\gamma\omega\nu\iota\alpha$, (topstone of the Pyramid)

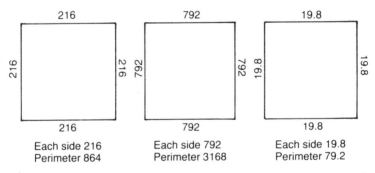

Each side 216   Each side 792   Each side 19.8
Perimeter 864   Perimeter 3168   Perimeter 79.2

When the diameters of the earth, sun and moon are stated in British miles they are multiples of creation's foundation number—12:

$$12 \times 72,000 = 864,000 \text{ (Sun)}$$
$$12 \times 660 = 7,920 \text{ (Earth)}$$
$$12 \times 180 = 2,160 \text{ (Moon)}$$

The harmony that we enjoy in music is based upon the wonderful numbers which are the building blocks of creation, and is related to the British mile unit. The number of vibrations per second in middle C is 264. The number of vibrations per second in C above middle C is 528, which is twice 264.

As already observed, the Station Stone Rectangle at Stonehenge bears the magnificent number 264, (side length,

264 feet). How appropriate to find that the gematria, or the numerical equivalent for "the truth," η αληθης, is 264. Middle C, "Do," when multiplied by the foundation number of all creation, equals 3168, which is the number for Lord Jesus Christ, Κυριος Ιησους Χριστος (12 × 264 = 3168).

The British mile unit, 5,280 feet, is part of the family which constitutes the building blocks of creation. Its relationship to music is found in C above middle C. This note, "Do," has 528 vibrations per second, and when played at the same time with middle C, flow together as one lovely harmonious note. When 528 is multiplied by one half of 12 the product is 3168— the numerical name for Lord Jesus Christ (6 × 528 = 3168).

The mile unit is subdivided into other units which are common to us: the foot, inch, yard, and furlong. The relationship of these units to other ancient linear units has been recorded for all the generations of man by the dimensions of Stonehenge.

1.76 feet = The great cubit
17.6 yards = The radius of the outer face of the Sarsen Circle
10.56 feet = The reed
10.56 feet = The mean length of each lintel of the Sarsen Circle
5,280 feet = The mile
52.8 feet = The radius of the outer face of the Sarsen Circle
19.8 inches = The Sumerian cubit
19.8 feet = The radius of the Bluestone Horseshoe
14,400 feet = The megalithic mile
144 feet = The radius of the Aubrey Circle

The royal cubit (1.72 feet) was the unit used in the construction of the Great Pyramid. The length of this unit in relation to the British system of linear measure is permanently recorded in the construction of the King's Chamber, whose width measures 17.2 feet.

1.72 feet = 1 Royal cubit
17.2 feet = Width of King's Chamber (10 royal cubits)

A list of all the linear units that will be used in subsequent chapters is as follows (given in relation to British measures):

THE MAGNIFICENT NUMBERS

12 inches = 1 foot
3 feet = 1 yard
660 feet = 1 furlong
5,280 feet = 1 mile
1.2165 feet = 1 remen
1.65 feet = 1 Sumerian cubit
1.72 feet = 1 royal cubit
1.76 feet = 1 great cubit
2.72 feet = 1 megalithic yard (MY)
10.56 feet = 1 reed
14,400 feet = 1 megalithic mile (MMi)
1.001064 inches = 1 Pyramid inch
25.0266 inches = 1 sacred cubit (25 Pyramid inches)

The modern metric system is related to none of these. It was contrived by man to represent one ten-millionth part of the length of a quadrant of the meridian through Paris; but it is not, in fact, commensurate with the universe and therefore is totally unsuitable for archaeological work and the measuring of antiquities.

The beautiful harmony in the numbers of all creation are, on the other hand, only possible because of the mile unit. If it had been devised by man, independent of a knowledge of the size of the sun, independent of a knowledge of the size of the earth and moon, and independent of the geometry and gematria of the Bible, then it would be the most colossial coincidence known to man!

All the evidence points away from coincidence, and toward some great magnificent plan, whose complexities and inter-relationships stagger the comprehension. We can only stand in awe—yes, even reverence—of such greatness!

We are able only to pull back the veil momentarily for a small glimpse of the vast secrets of the universe and of time. But the limitless unknown still lies beyond our view.

The Wonderful Numberer surely was a Numberer of Secrets. And it has become apparent that divine secrets do indeed have numbers—magnificent numbers. The word ''secret'' in

Hebrew is בסוד, and bears the number 72. A square with sides of 72 has a perimeter of 288.

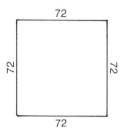

Each side, 72 — Secret, בסוד, 72
Perimeter, 288 — Base Perimeter of Pyramid, 288 reeds

The square defines the base perimeter of the Great Pyramid, which measures 288 reeds. There has never been a more profound secret than the mystery of the Great Pyramid. Its four sides speak to us the words secret, secret, secret, secret! And the darkness that lies within has hidden its secrets for 4,000 years. Much has been discovered regarding the origin and purpose of that most ancient wonder of the world, yet they are only surfaces if we are to ignore the grandeur of its architect.

Emerson once said "Nothing is rich but the inexhaustible wealth of nature. She shows us only surfaces, but she is a million fathoms deep."

Zophar, one of Job's would-be comforters, attempted to express our limited knowledge of the mysteries of the universe and of the Creator:

"But oh that God would speak, and open his lips...and that he would show thee the secrets of wisdom, that they are double to that which is." (Job 11:5, 6).

The front (north) face of the Great Pyramid showing the original gabled entrance. Al Mamoun's forced entrance is in the lower right.

4

The Temple on the Rock

The year was about 1991 B.C.; it was a lonely, desert land through which four travelers passed—a father, his beloved son, and two hired servants. After three days they arrived at their destination—a rocky hill in the land of Moriah. The father and son, carrying wood for a fire, proceeded to the top of the hill, while the two servants waited with the pack animals in the valley below.

The father was heavy of heart, and silent, as he walked slowly up the rocky slope; the son, in silence, following. It had been apparent that his father was preparing to offer a sacrifice to his God, but the young man was puzzled, and so he broke the silence. "My father...behold the fire and the wood, but where is the lamb for a burnt offering?"

The question cut to the heart of the old man. Three days before, he had heard a voice in a dream telling him to come to this place, telling him to offer his beloved son in sacrifice. The voice had been the voice of God. Now the moment had arrived, and he must obey. He dared not look at the handsome young man, remembering how he had dandled him on his knees when he was just a child, how he had watched the boy grow. He dared not think how desperately he loved him. He continued to look to the rocky plateau atop the hill, and as they walked together he replied quietly, "My son, God will provide himself a lamb."

Reaching the top of the hill, the old man built an altar on the rock, and laid the wood in place upon the altar. Then, trying to blot out the feelings that were crying out from within his heart,

THE MAGNIFICENT NUMBERS

Painting by Marjorie Rice - Photo by Thomas Gilbert

Today the Mosque of Omar stands on the rock where Abraham offered Isaac.

he bound the young man and placed him on the altar. He pulled his knife from its sheath, and raised it above that beloved body, trying not to look at the dear eyes which looked so pleadingly, yet silently, up at him.

But as he, trembling, held the knife, he heard a voice call to him: "Abraham, Abraham!"

He recognized the voice. It was the same voice that had spoken to him in the dream three days previously. The voice continued, "Lay not thine hand upon the lad...for now I know that thou fearest God, seeing thou hast not withheld thy son, thine only son from me."

Abraham was stunned with joy and relief. And in his haste to untie his son and hold him close to his breast, he saw a ram, whose horns had been caught in a thicket. He took the ram and offered it on the altar as a sacrifice to his God, in the place of his son, Isaac.

From out of the depths of deepest grief, up into sublime joy, Abraham called the name of the place Jehovah-jireh—"The mount of the Lord."

The name bears the same number as the Wonderful Numberer, Palmoni. Jehovah יהוה, 26 — jireh יראה, 216.

The rocky summit of Mount Moriah has, for thousands of years, been referred to simply as the "Rock." It has come to be universally known as the place of union between God and man.

Long after the time of Abraham, one of his descendents, King David, purchased this Rock from a man named Arunah (Ornan). David had talked with a heavenly messenger who was standing on the Rock, and afterward was impelled to offer sacrifice there—a sacrifice of thanksgiving.

Later, David's son, Solomon, built a temple there. This Rock, situated on the top of Mount Moriah, had long been regarded as the most sacred spot to the Jewish people. It was the meeting place between God and man.

After Solomon's temple was burned by Nebuchadnezzar in 586 B.C., the Rock lay desolate until the return of the Jews from their Babylonian exile, when, under the leadership of Zerubabbel, another temple was built upon it.

In 21 B.C., Herod the Great, who ruled the land of Judea under Caesar Augustus of Rome, built a third temple on the ruins of the second temple. This beautiful and imposing edifice was destroyed by the army of Titus in A.D. 70—Rome's seige of Jerusalem. The only thing that remained was a portion of a retaining wall, now known as the Wailing Wall, or Western Wall. It is a sacred spot for the Jewish people for it is reminiscent of their communion with God in the days of their monarchy.

In A.D. 637 the Caliph Omar built a temporary structure upon the Rock, to be followed in A.D. 738 by the beautiful mosque which remains to this day—the Mosque of Omar, better known as the Dome of the Rock. The floor of the inner chamber of this mosque is the Rock—the rock where Abraham offered his son, Isaac, in sacrifice. This mosque, to every Arab, is sacred; to every Jew it defiles the temple site.

The Rock was, in fact, the foundation for each of the structures that had been built upon it. This Rock that is sacred to both Jew and Arab, is also known as the Foundation.

The temple which Solomon built was the meeting place between God and man in the days of the Jewish monarchy. It was a *sign* to them that their kingdom was a kingdom under God.

Certainly this was one of the *signs* of which Jeremiah spoke:

"The Great, the Mighty God, the Lord of Hosts is his name...which hast set signs and wonders in the land of Egypt, even to this day, and in Israel, and among other men." (Jeremiah 32:18-20)

How do we know that the temple was the "sign" in Israel? It has been demonstrated that the Great Pyramid and Stonehenge were signs and wonders, and it can likewise be demonstrated that the temple is the third sign to which Jeremiah referred.

The beautiful temple which Solomon built upon the Rock on Mount Moriah measured 20 by 60 cubits. It had two main rooms—the Most Holy, which had a base perimeter of 20×20 cubits, and the Holy, whose base perimeter was 20×40 cubits. The base perimeter of the two rooms would thus be 160 cubits. And how appropriate that they should be built upon the Rock, for the Hebrew word for rock, צלם, has the numerical equivalent of 160.

The Rock also went by the common appellation of the Foundation, which in Hebrew is יסד, and bears the number 74. The number 74 is indeed a foundation number—it is one of the building blocks of all creation. The word creation in Greek, κτισις, is 740. The Creator, who is called in the Old Testament, *Elohim,* bears the number 86. How thrilling to find that $86 + 74 = 160$, which is the Rock, the Foundation, the meeting place between God and man.

The base perimeter of the temple was 160 cubits, but what cubit was used? In II Chronicles 3:3 it is stated:

Now these are the things wherein Solomon was instructed for the building of the house of God. The length by cubits after the first measure *was threescore cubits, and the breadth twenty cubits.*

The Revised Standard Version translates this: *"the length in cubits of the old standard."* The cubit of the old standard, the one that had been used in ancient Israel, was one that they had acquired from the people of Sumer. The Sumerians used the cubit of 19.8 inches. Through the years Israel had come to use a longer cubit, the royal cubit, an Egyptian measure. However, the chronicler made it clear that the cubit of the *"old standard"* was the one used in the construction of the temple.

The 160 cubits of the perimeter of the temple, when multiplied by 19.8 inches, equals 3168 inches, and, as has been demonstrated, the name Lord Jesus Christ, $K\upsilon\rho\iota o\varsigma\ 'I\eta\sigma o\upsilon\varsigma\ X\rho\iota\sigma\tau o\varsigma$, is 3168. He is called the Rock; he is also called the Foundation.

There are two words in the Hebrew Old Testament translated rock. The second word is צור, and bears the number 296. What a beautiful harmony! A square with sides of 74 has a perimeter of 296.

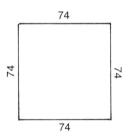

Each side 74— Foundation, יסד 74
Perimeter 296— Rock, רוצ 296
Only Begotten, $\mu o\nu o\gamma\varepsilon\nu\eta$ 296

In John 3:16 are recorded the beautiful words:

For God so loved the world that he gave his only begotten son, that whosoever believeth in him should not perish, but have everlasting life.

THE MAGNIFICENT NUMBERS

The title *Only Begotten,* μονογενη, is 296. When 296 is multiplied by the number that represents Jesus, 8, the product is 2368, which is the gematria for Jesus Christ.

$$8 \times 296 = 2368 \text{ Jesus Christ } \text{'I}ησους \ X ριστος.$$

It is not by coincidence that he should be represented by the number that is the Rock, the Foundation of the temple. It was part of a great design. When Abraham offered his son in sacrifice on the Rock, it was indeed a picture, pointing to and representing the great sacrifice of Jehovah—the giving of his only begotten son. The Rock becomes the focal point in the salvation of man! And it was not by coincidence that Jesus was crucified on Mount Moriah (Calvary was part of Moriah).

The name Calvary in Greek is *Kranion,* which means a skull. The gematria for *Kranion,* κρανιον, is 301. A square with sides of 301 has a perimeter of 1204, which is the gematria for *"The holy mount at Jerusalem"* (Isaiah 27:13), בדר הקדש בירושלם.

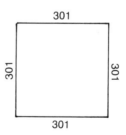

Each side, 301 — Calvary, κρανιον, 301
Perimeter, 1204 — The Holy Mount at Jerusalem,
בדר הקדש בירושלם,1204

The name Abraham in the New Testament is Αβρααμ, 144 (145).[1] A square with sides of 144 has a perimeter of 576. Surely the temple built upon the Rock was one of the *wonders* (576) of which Jeremiah spoke.

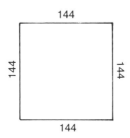

Each side 144— Abraham, 144 Αβρααμ
Perimeter 576— Wonders, 576 ונמפתים

In the New Testament we are introduced to a happy word—a word which means *good news*. The word is *gospel*. How appropriate that gospel, ευαγγελιον, should bear the number 576. The three wonders (576)—the Great Pyramid, Stonehenge and the temple tell a story of good news, for they tell of a redeemer who would save mankind from a dying condition and give them life.

This good news (gospel, 576) was embodied in the hope of a kingdom. The Jews in Jesus' day expected that he would restore to them their monarchy under God. But Jesus taught them concerning a future kingdom, which he called the Kingdom of God. This kingdom for which he taught his disciples to pray bears the number 1152.

576 = Wonders, ונמפתים
576 = Gospel, ευαγγελιον
1152 = Kingdom of God, την βασιλειαν Θεου
2 × 576 = 1152

[1] In gematria, one or two units, known as colel, may be added to or subtracted from the value of any word without affecting its meaning.

Jesus taught his disciples that this gospel of the Kingdom of God should be proclaimed throughout the world for a witness.

576 = Gospel, ευαγγελιον
2 × 576 = 1152, Kingdom of God, την βασιλειαν Θεου
576 + 1152 = 1728, Proclaim, κηρυσσω
1152 = Witness, μαρτυριας

The temple that was built upon the Rock was a symbol of that Kingdom of God. It was the meeting place between God and man.

The prophet Isaiah wrote of that future kingdom: *"A king shall reign in righteousness."* Then he referred to that king as being like *"the shadow of a great rock in a weary land."* (Isaiah 32:1 & 2)

This king, the *"Great Rock"* סלע כבד, has a number value of 186. Golgotha also has the number value of 186. The name Golgotha means "the skull," and the hill was appropriately named, for the caves in the sides of the rock do indeed give it the appearance of a skull. It was on this Rock that the only begotten son of God was put to death by crucifixion. Thus the number 186 is found to represent both death and life.

186 = Golgotha, Γολγοθα
186 = Great Rock, סלע כבד
(26 = Great)
(160 = Rock)

The Rock is used throughout both the Old and New Testaments as a metaphor relating to the foundation of the faith of the Christian. The number values of the texts using this concept clearly relate to Jesus. One of the titles which he applied to himself was *"The Way"*—he said; *"I am the Way, the Truth, and the Life."* The number value for The Way, η οδος, is 352. It is not by coincidence that King David prayed to *"The God of my Rock,"* אלהי צורי, whose number value is 352. Nor is it coincidence that a square with sides of 352 has a perimeter of 1408, which is the number value for Saviour, σωτηρ.

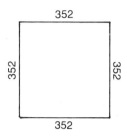

One side 352— The Way, η οδος, 352
The God of my Rock, אלהי צורי, 352
Perimeter 1408— Savior, σωτηρ, 1408

In this prayer of King David, recorded in II Samuel 22:3, are found the beautiful words, *"The God of my Rock, he is my shield, and the horn of my salvation, my high tower, and my refuge."* And equally as beautiful are the numerical relationships hidden within the text.

My Refuge, רמנוסי = 172
(God, 86 × 2 = 172)
(1.72 feet = 1 Royal Cubit)
(17.2 feet = width of King's Chamber and
                Queen's Chamber in Pyramid)

"He is my shield, and the horn of my salvation, my high tower and my refuge." מגני וקרן ישעי משגבי ומנוסי = 1376
(8 × 172 = 1376)
(16 × 86 = 1376)

"The God of my Rock, he is my shield, and the horn of my salvation, my high tower, and my refuge."
אלהי צורי מגני וקרן ישעי משגבי ומנוסי = 1728
(2 × 1728 = 3456 — 4 × 864 = 3456)
(2 × 864 = 1728 — Diameter of sun, 864,000 miles)
(8 × 216 = 1728 — Diameter of moon, 2160 miles)
(4 × 432 = 1728 — Radius of sun, 432,000 miles)
(3 × 576 = 1728 — Gospel, 576; Wonders, 576)
(6 × 288 = 1728 — Perimeter of Pyramid, 288 reeds; Diameter of
                Aubrey Circle, 288 feet)
(12 × 144 = 1728 — Perimeter of New Jerusalem, 144,000 furlongs)

THE MAGNIFICENT NUMBERS

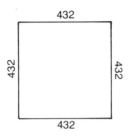

Each side 432— Radius of Sun 432,000 miles
Perimeter 1728— II Samuel 22:3 = 1728
אלהי צורי מגני וקרן ישעי משגבי
ומנוסי

The solar number, 864, and the lunar number, 216, play an interesting role in relation to the number values of the prayer of King David, as well as their relationship to the temple on the Rock. The Hebrew word for rock is 160, and a square with sides of 160 has a perimeter of 640, which is the number value for the Hebrew word *sun,* שמש.

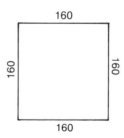

Each side 160— Rock, צלס, 160
Perimeter 640— Sun, שמש, 640

There are two Hebrew words used in the Old Testament for sun. The other word is חמה, which has a number value of 54. A square with sides of 54 has a perimeter of 216 (the lunar number).

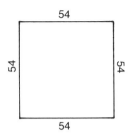

Each side 54— Sun, חמה, 54
Perimeter 216— Diameter of Moon 2,160 miles

When the number values of the two Hebrew words *sun* are multiplied they equal the square drawn on the sun as shown below:

$$\text{Sun} = 54$$
$$\text{Sun} = 640$$
$$54 \times 640 = 34560$$

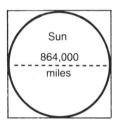

Perimeter of square 3,456,000 miles

It was surely not a coincidence that at Stonehenge, the Station Stone Rectangle, in inches, is the magnificent number 3456. The architect of that amazing monument—a monument that points directly toward the rising of the sun—knew the beautiful solar relationship of the number 3456.

The product of these four numbers is the number of degrees in a circle (3 x 4 x 5 x 6 = 360). Who originated the concept of 360° in a circle? Its origins cannot be traced to man; yet it has come down to us from ancient times and has been universally used without question. It was planted in the great circle of the heavens by the 12 divisions of the Zodiac. This Zodiacal year of 360 days was used by the writers of the Old Testament as the length of the prophetic year. The time prophecies of the Bible are all based upon the 360-day year. The 12 divisions of the Zodiac are incorporated into the design of the Sarsen Circle at Stonehenge, for the circle is divided into 30 equal parts of 12° by the 30 upright sarsen stones.

The architect of Stonehenge and the Great Pyramid demonstrated an intimate knowledge of the geometry of the universe. The ancient philosopher and mathematician, Pythagoras, gave us the concept of the geometry of the right triangle. His theorem of the 3:4:5 triangle has come down to us as the single most important theorem in the whole of mathematics because by it he established the fundamental characterization of time and space, and the laws that bind the universe. Pythagoras discovered a great truth, but the application of that truth was planted in the universe from the beginning of creation.

The architect of the Great Pyramid designed its proportions to conform to the geometrical relationships of the earth and moon. We have shown in Figure 6 the construction of a pyramid on the diameter and combined radii of the earth and moon, whose proportions are identical to the Great Pyramid. With that same illustration, let's draw squares around the earth and moon as in Figure 14 below.

Note that the combined radii of earth and moon is 5,040 miles, which is the product of the progression of 2, 3, 4, 5, 6, 7.

$$2 \times 3 \times 4 \times 5 \times 6 \times 7 = 5040$$
$$14 \times 360 = 5040$$

The right triangle formed by the position of the squares is a 3:4:5 triangle—but not just any 3:4:5 triangle. Look at its dimensions! Its height is of course equal to the diameter of the moon, but its base is the magnificent number which defines the perimeter of both Stonehenge and the Great Pyramid.[2] Thus the hypotenuse becomes the number that defines both time and space—360. Pythagoras was right; numbers do indeed seem to be the language of the universe!

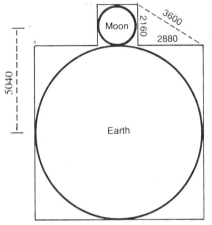

Perimeter of joining squares, 36,000 miles

FIGURE 14

The diameter of the earth, sun and moon are multiples of the number 360:

Diameter of sun ....864,000 miles
                                            (2400 × 360)
Diameter of earth ....7,920 miles
                                            (22 × 360)
Diameter of moon................................2,160 miles
                                            (9 × 360)

---

[2]The magnificent number which defines the perimeter of both Stonehenge and the Great Pyramid is 288. The *"Kingdom of Heaven,"* βασιλεια των ουρνων, also bears the number 2880.

The height of a pyramid constructed on the combined radii of the earth and moon is 5040 units, and it is interesting to note that another reference to the *"Kingdom of Heaven"* in Revelation 11:15, *"The Kingdom of our Lord and of His Christ,"* βασιλεα Κυριου ημων και Χριστου αυτου, equals 5040.

The perimeters of the squares on the earth and moon as shown in the diagram above are also part of the magnificent numbers of the Great Pyramid and Stonehenge.

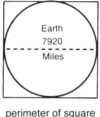

perimeter of square
31,680 miles

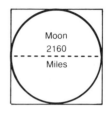

perimeter of square
8,640 miles

The dimensions of the temple on the Rock were not chosen arbitrarily by King Solomon. They were given to him by his God, the God who had instructed Abraham to offer his son in sacrifice on this same Rock. If the specifications for the temple had been by human design, we would have much cause to wonder and to marvel, for they not only reveal a knowledge of the man, Jesus Christ, a thousand years before his time, but they also reveal a knowledge of the universe—the geometry relating to the earth, sun and moon, at a time when such accurate knowledge was not available to man. We are not left to conjecture, however, regarding the architect. The Bible clearly states that it was the design of the Almighty. The interrelationship of the temple with the gematria of the Bible and the geometry of the Great Pyramid and Stonehenge leads to a logical hypothesis—God, the author of the Bible and the architect of the temple also fits the requirements for the architect of the Pyramid and Stonehenge. Surely the Creator of the earth, sun and moon knew their precise dimensions—knowledge that was not to be known by man until comparatively modern times.

Wherever we look in the temple we can find its relationship to the universe, the gematria of the Bible, and the geometry of Stonehenge and the Great Pyramid. This "sign" and "witness" in the land of Israel was truly a "wonder."

The temple was divided into two principal rooms, the Holy and the Most Holy. The geometry of the floor plan alone is replete with the magnificent numbers. The Most Holy measured 20 cubits by 20 cubits, making a base perimeter of 80 cubits, or 132 feet. The table below demonstrates the beauty of the number 132:

$132 \times 2 = 264$
    264 feet = long side of the Station Stone Rectangle
    26.4 yards = diameter of Bluestone Circle
    264 = The Truth, $\eta\ \alpha\lambda\eta\theta\eta\varsigma$

$132 \times 3 = 396$
    39.6 feet = diameter of Bluestone Horseshoe
    39.6 feet = radius of Bluestone Circle
    3960 miles = radius of earth
    396 MMi = radius of moon

$132 \times 4 = 528$
    52.8 feet = radius of outer face of Sarsen Circle
    52.8 yards = perimeter of square drawn on the
                       Bluestone Horseshoe
    5280 feet = one British mile

$132 \times 5 = 660$
    660 feet = one furlong

$132 \times 6 = 792$
    79.2 feet = diameter of Bluestone Circle
    7920 miles = diameter of earth
    792 MMi = diameter of moon

$132 \times 8 = 1056$
    10.56 feet = mean length of each lintel of the Sarsen Circle
    105.6 feet = diameter of outer face of Sarsen Circle
    105.6 yards = mean circumference of Sarsen Circle
    10.56 feet = one Reed
    1056 = *The joy of thy salvation* (Psalm 51:12) ששׂון ישׂעֶךָ

$132 \times 9 = 1188$
    1188 = *Glory of God,* $\delta o\xi\alpha\ \tau o\upsilon\ \Theta\varepsilon o\upsilon$

$132 \times 12 = 1584$
    1584 = *Priests of God,* (I Corinthians 12:14) $\iota\varepsilon\rho\varepsilon\iota\ \tau o\upsilon\ \Theta\varepsilon o\upsilon$

$132 \times 15 = 1980$
    19.8 feet = radius of Bluestone Horseshoe
    19.8 inches = one Sumerian cubit

$132 \times 16 = 2112$
    2112 = *A virgin shall conceive and bear a son, and shall call his name Immanuel,*
                                               העלמה הרה וילדת בן וקראת שמו עמנו אל
                (Isaiah 7:4)

$132 \times 24 = 3168$
    316.8 feet = mean circumference of Sarsen Circle
    3168 inches = long side of Station Stone Rectangle
    31,680 furlongs = radius of earth
    316,800 MMi = diameter of sun
    3168 = Lord Jesus Christ, $K\upsilon\rho\iota o\varsigma$ ᾽$I\eta\sigma o\upsilon\varsigma$ $X\rho\iota\sigma\tau o\varsigma$
    31,680 feet = 6 miles

When this same type of computation is done with the base perimeter of the Holy (20 × 40 cubits) most of the significant numbers are repeated, *i.e.*, 396, 792, 1188, 1584, 1980, 3168.

Continue the same computation with the combined Holy and Most Holy, and again the significant numbers are repeated, *i.e.*, 264, 528, 792, 1056, 1584, 2112, 3168, 3960.

Now let's consider each side of the base:

20 cubits = 396 inches
    3960 miles = radius of earth
40 cubits = 792 inches
    7920 miles = diameter of earth
60 cubits = 1188 inches
    1188 = *Glory of God,* $\delta o\xi\alpha$ $\tau o\upsilon$ $\Theta\varepsilon o\upsilon$

The base perimeter of the temple is unique in that it is evenly divisible not only by the British linear units, but also by the great cubit and the reed.

Temple base perimeter:

160 Sumerian cubits	88 Yards
264 British feet	150 Great cubits
3168 Inches	25 Reeds

THE TEMPLE ON THE ROCK

It is most appropriate that the gematria for *"glory of God"* is found in the foundation of the temple, for surely the simple, yet unique geometry of that beautiful edifice—the *"wonder in the land of Egypt"*—reveals the glory of a supreme intelligence.

It seems evident that the same intelligence directed the design of the Great Pyramid and Stonehenge. These *"wonders in Egypt...and among other men"* truly take their rightful place among the ancient wonders of the world.

Photo by Robert Alexander

Stonehenge in the early morning mist. This 4,000-year-old edifice is truly one of the wonders of the ancient world.

The front, or north face of the Great Pyramid.

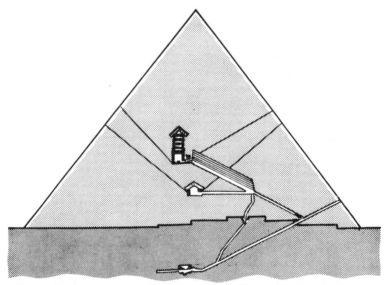

The vertical meridian section of the Great Pyramid, showing its passage and chamber system.

5

A Tomb or a Temple?

The possibility that the Great Pyramid was more than a tomb has haunted the minds of all who have profoundly studied this age-enduring structure.

Historians are nearly all in agreement that no one was, in fact, ever buried there. Many suppose it to have been built for the purpose of entombing the body of the Egyptian king Cheops, but Egyptologists inform us that he was buried in an elaborately-cut sepulcher about a thousand feet away from the Pyramid.

Joseph A. Seiss wrote in 1877:[1]

Helfricus (1565) and Baumgarten (1594) considered the Great Pyramid a tomb, but held that no one was ever buried in it. Pietro Della Valle (1616), Thevenot (1655), and Maillet (1692) give it as the common belief that no one ever was therein entombed. Shaw (1721) denies that it ever was a tomb or ever was intended to be one. Mr. St. John does not consider the coffer a sarcophagus at all, and thinks the Great Pyramid never was, and never was meant to be a tomb.

Seiss continues with his own observation and convictions:[2]

The truth is that the tomb theory does not fit the facts, the traditions, or any knowledge that we have on the subject. It is wholly borrowed from the numerous later pyramids,

---

[1] Joseph A. Seiss, *Miracle in Stone,* The Castle Press, Philadelphia, 1877, p. 183.

[2] *Ibid.,* p. 185

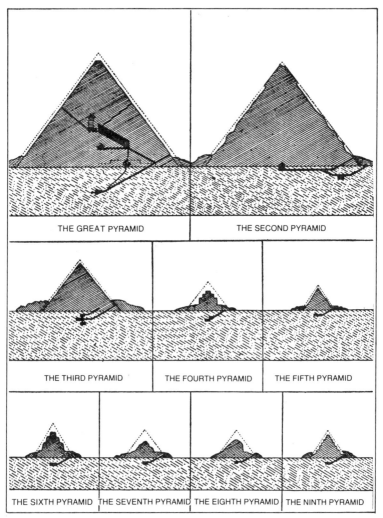

THE GREAT PYRAMID

THE SECOND PYRAMID

THE THIRD PYRAMID

THE FOURTH PYRAMID

THE FIFTH PYRAMID

THE SIXTH PYRAMID

THE SEVENTH PYRAMID

THE EIGHTH PYRAMID

THE NINTH PYRAMID

The above is an adaptation of the drawings of Piazzi Smyth showing the vertical meridian section of the nine pyramids of Gizeh. Note that all have descending passages, but the Great Pyramid, alone, has ascending passages. These upper passages were sealed and hidden by the builders, hence those who attempted to copy the design knew only of the descending passage.

ambitiously and ignorantly copied after it, which *were* intended and used for royal sepulchres, but with which the Great Pyramid has nothing in common, save locality and general shape. In all the examination to which it has been subjected, whether in ancient or modern times, and in all the historic fragments concerning it, there is nothing whatever to give or to bear out the idea that its intention was that of a royal sepulchral monument, or that can legitimately raise the tomb theory any higher than a possible, but very improbable *supposition.*

The ''numerous later pyramids'' to which Seiss has reference, are about thirty-eight in all, and they dot the western side of the Nile along the edge of the great Sahara Desert. All of them are square-based, with four triangular sloping sides meeting at the top in a point over the center of the base. They are all smaller and inferior in quality and workmanship to the Great Pyramid. Many of them have long since collapsed into rounded ruins and are no longer recognizable as pyramids. They all, with the exception of the Great Pyramid, have one thing in common: they have no upper passages and chambers.

Why would all the other pyramids have only descending passages and subterranean chambers? If they all were designed to be tombs, and if they all were copies of the Great Pyramid, would they not have upper passages and chambers?

When the Caliph Al Mamoun and his workmen forced an entrance into the dark interior of the Great Pyramid in A.D. 820 they found only a descending passage. However, the pounding of their hammers dislodged a large limestone block that had hidden the entrance to the upper chambers. The block had obviously been placed there by the builders to prevent the intrusion into the ascending passage, as well as to hide all knowledge of its existence. And as if this were not enough, they filled the bottom portion of the ascending passage with not one, but *three,* tight-fitting granite plugs.

The builders of the other pyramids had no knowledge of the ascending passages and chambers above. They only had access to the descending passage and the subterranean chamber. (The original entrance to the descending passage, had, at that time, not yet been hidden.)

There is positive evidence in some of the lesser pyramids that they were used for tombs, and had been built specifically for that purpose. No such evidence has ever been found at the Great Pyramid.

As Al Mamoun and his men penetrated the darkness of the upper passages and chambers, they found them totally empty, save for centuries of bat dung. The granite box in the King's Chamber was empty, and no lid has ever been found for it. If there had been a lid, it could not have been removed, for the passageways were too small for its transport. It could not have been broken into small pieces and removed, for there would have been no way to transport the necessary tools through the passages and into the King's Chamber. No passage was at all possible through the first ascending passageway, because of the three granite plugs. The only possible means of access would have been to ascend the well shaft. However, this small vertical shaft was completely blocked with dirt, debris and bat dung. It was not made possible to traverse until opened in the early 1800s by Captain G. B. Caviglia.

Even after the well shaft was cleared of rubble left by the builders, it was nearly impossible to ascend. To climb the dark steep and narrow shaft required the support of a rope dropped from above. Even if this shaft had been left open at the time of the completion of construction, subsequent marauders would have required support from above to climb it, and would have had the insuperable task of transporting their tools upward; then they would have had to break up the theoretical lid of the granite box, and retrace the same route, back down through the impossibly narrow, steep well—an engineering feat unrivaled even by the forced entrance of Al Mamoun. And, I might add, if such marauders desired to remove a mummy they would have had to use the same procedure, which, at this point, obviously becomes a self-defeating hypothesis.

No! It never contained a mummy; and the granite coffer never had a lid! For what purpose, then, was this magnificent structure built?

The awesomeness of the size and antiquity of this beautiful edifice has intrigued the minds of men for thousands of years. Its structural durability has surpassed all others. No one can contemplate this mighty structure, built four thousand years ago, without standing in awe of its beauty of masonry, its exclusiveness of design both externally and internally, and the masterly workmanship of its builders. None of the subsequent stone edifices can vie with the Great Pyramid in fineness of workmanship.

Professor C. Piazzi Smyth, in his book *The Antiquity of Intellectual Man,* comments upon the closeness of the masonry joints of the building, and particularly the construction of the walls of the Queen's Chamber.

The joints are so close, that the edges of the two surfaces of worked stone, and the filling of cement between, are comprisable often within the thickness of a hair.

The renouned Professor Wm. Flinders Petrie observed:

To merely place such stones in exact contact at the sides would be careful work [because the stones are so large and heavy], but to do so with cement in the joints seems almost impossible.

Later, commenting on the marvellous skill of the workmen in the placing of the casing stones, Petrie said:

Their skill in cementing joints is hard to understand. How, in the casing of the Great Pyramid, they could fill with cement a vertical joint about 5 feet by 7 feet in area, and only averaging one-fiftieth part of an inch thickness is a mystery; more especially as the joint could not be thinned by rubbing, owing to its being a vertical joint, and the blocks weighing about 16 tons. Yet this was the usual work over 13 acres of surface, with tens of thousands of casing stones, none less than a ton in weight.

The workmanship alone staggers the comprehension, but its design reveals an intelligence superior to that of man. The noted Pyramidologist, Morton Edgar, after many years of exploration and research, wrote concerning this great edifice:[3]

Built nearly five and a half centuries before the tabernacle of Moses was erected in the wilderness, and twice as long before the temple of David and Solomon appeared in Jerusalem (and both of these edifices were designed under Divine inspiration), the Great Pyramid has withstood the ravages of all centuries till now, and will probably continue to stand for many more, testifying to earth's inhabitants the omnipotence of Jehovah. Completed two decades before Abraham was born, it held hidden within its measures and angles a prophetic history of the world, not decipherable until history had run its course.

In addition, it contains, by means of its design and proportionate dimensions, important scientific facts, which never could be appreciated until precise knowledge of the laws which govern movement in the universe had sufficiently increased, to prepare the mind of man to unlock them.

The King's Chamber (see illustration on page 5) and its mysterious open granite coffer contain basic scientific truths which have come down to us as fundamental principles of mathematics. We have observed (page 61) that the Pythagorean 3:4:5 triangle was planted in the dimensions of the earth and moon by the Creator. The same proportions were planted in the King's Chamber by its architect.

Using the measurements of Professor Smyth, Mr. James Simpson of Edinburgh, Scotland, was first to perceive this remarkable proportion. He observed that the end-wall diagonal is (proportionately) 3, the length of the chamber 4, and the cubic diagonal 5. These dimensions represent the height, base, and

---

[3] Morton Edgar, *The Great Pyramid, Its Scientific Features,* MacClure, MacDonald & Co., Glasgow, 1924, pp. 14, 15.

hypotenuse of a right triangle, respectively. He also saw that one-half of the chamber's width, when taken as a unit of measure, gives the proportionate measures of all parts of the chamber, through the multiplication of square roots thus:

Half the chamber's width × square root of 4 gives width

"	"	×	"	5 gives height
"	"	×	"	9 gives end diagonal
"	"	×	"	16 gives length
"	"	×	"	20 gives floor diagonal
"	"	×	"	21 gives side diagonal
"	"	×	"	25 gives cubic diagonal
			Total	100

Based upon these beautiful proportions, the standard dimensions of the King's Chamber, generally accepted by Pyramidologists are:

Length	412.13168792	Pyramid inches
Width	206.0658439604	"
Height	230.3886174681	"
Floor diagonal	460.7772349363	"
Side diagonal	472.1561640467	"
End diagonal	309.0987659406	"
Cubic diagonal	515.164609010	"

(2 × width = length)
(2 × height = floor diagonal)
(width + end diagonal = cubic diagonal)

Not only has the 3:4:5 triangle been monumentalized in stone, the true length of the ancient royal cubit has similarly been permanently recorded by the width of the King's Chamber, for it is 10 royal cubits, or 17.2 feet. The width of this chamber, in Pyramid inches, multiplied by the square root of π is 365.242198, or exactly the number of days in the solar tropical year.

Now the above facts, at first glance, may sound like a bit of mathematical hocus-pocus. But let's take a second look.

THE MAGNIFICENT NUMBERS

All the dimensions of the King's Chamber are proportioned to its width through the medium of square roots. And additionally we find that the actual width measurement is proportioned to the day-value of the year through the medium of a square root, and a highly scientific one at that—the square root of π.

Bear in mind that the unit used for this calculation, the Pyramid inch, is based upon the actual size of the earth; an even 500,000,000 such inches make up the length of the earth's polar axis of rotation. As the earth revolves once around its axis it marks off the duration of one day, and during the time it takes to complete its orbit around the sun it has revolved on its axis 365.242198 times—it has completed one solar tropical year. All this scientific data was built into the Pyramid's principal chamber, the King's Chamber. The proportions of that granite-walled room have monumentalized for all the ages of man the value of the 3:4:5 right triangle, the ratio of π, and the length of the solar tropical year. The possibilities of these facts being known by any man 4,000 years ago, without the aid of a higher intelligence, are remote indeed—perhaps impossible. What man, in that era of our ancient past, knew the polar axial diameter of the earth? Only man's Creator!

Earth's equitorial semi-axis - 3,963.5303 miles
Earth's polar semi-axis - 3,950.1833 miles
Ratio - 297:296

74

The earth is not a perfect sphere, it is flattened at the poles and bulges at the equator. Consequently, a great circle at the poles is not, in fact, a circle—it more resembles an elipse; thus the polar axial diameter differs in length from the equatorial diameter by the ratio of 296 to 297. The architect of the Great Pyramid knew this proportion, for based upon this unique proportion, the Pyramid reveals its own location—its precise latitude. This remarkable fact was first discovered by Herbert L. Prout in 1933. It gives firm evidence of the divine origin of this most remarkable edifice.

The proportion works like this: if we projected an imaginary line extending from the Pyramid's entrance passage, out into space, it would intersect earth's axis of rotation at a distance exactly seven earth-diameters away from the center of the earth. If the Pyramid had been built even 100 feet away from its site, or if the passage angle were minutely different, or if the earth were a fraction larger or smaller, this remarkable property would be lost.

The entrance passage of the Great Pyramid becomes a pointer, pin-pointing its precise location on the face of the earth. If this pointer was indeed intended as a key to its exact geographical position, then whoever picked the site for its erection was cognizant of the *true* shape of the earth.

The architect who designed the angle of the

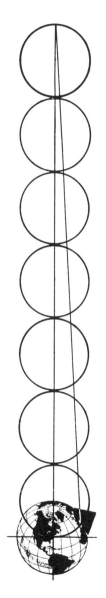

passages in the Great Pyramid displayed a remarkable know-ledge of mathematics. All of the inclined passages slope at the same steep angle of 26° 18′ 9.7″. The sine of this angle is equal to the square root of π divided by 4.

$$\text{sine of } 26° 18′ 9.7″ = .4431135$$
$$\frac{\sqrt{\pi}}{4} = .4431135$$

The peculiar angle of 26° 18′ 9.7″ reveals the exact length of earth's solar tropical year. If we were to measure off on the floor line of any of the angle passages a portion equal to twice the length of the King's Chamber, and regard this section as the hypotenuse of a right triangle, the perpendicular of that triangle would be as many Pyramid inches as there are days in the solar tropical year, *i.e.*, 365.242.

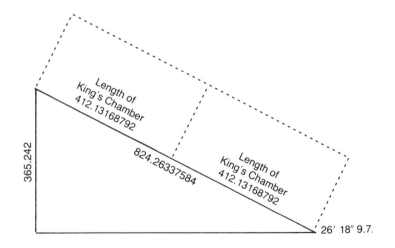

FIGURE 15

76

Having ruled out coincidence, what else is left? Reason can only conclude that it was intelligent design. Magnificent intelligent design! But why such a steep angle? Why this particular angle?

This unique angle of the passageways not only reveals the Pyramid's key to its own geographical location, and the length of the solar tropical year, it reveals a distinct relationship to Stonehenge and the actual size of the earth. It is, in fact, based upon the dimensions of earth and can be constructed by the use of the circles of Stonehenge.

Consider 79.2 feet as the radius of a circle; now draw a square tangent to the circle. This is the relationship of the Bluestone Circle to the Sarsen Circle at Stonehenge. Square the circle and each side of the resultant square will measure 140.378 feet. Now stack the squares in the manner shown below, and the angle created is precisely the Pyramid passage angle—26° 18′ 9.7″.

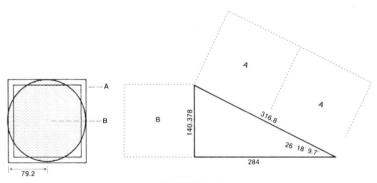

FIGURE 16

When we realize that the Great Pyramid was completed prior to the erecting of Stonehenge, we stand in awe of such a demonstration of geometry. Unmistakably, the dimensions of both structures were built upon the mean diameter of the earth. And this unusual angle of 26° 18′ 9.7″ shows beyond reasonable doubt that one architect was involved in both monuments. And, whoever he was, he had an intimate knowledge of the universe.

THE MAGNIFICENT NUMBERS

The right triangle demonstrated above bears a remarkable set of numbers. The base measures 284 feet, and the hypotenuse is 316.8 feet. The hypotenuse is, in fact, identical in length to the mean circumference of the Sarsen Circle. But it is much more!

It is surely not coincidence that the hypotenuse of this unique triangle bears the number 3168, which is the gematria for Lord Jesus Christ, Κυριος Ιησους Χριστος, and that the base bears the number 284, which is the gematria for God, Θεος. (The

The Christ Angle
in the Great Pyramid

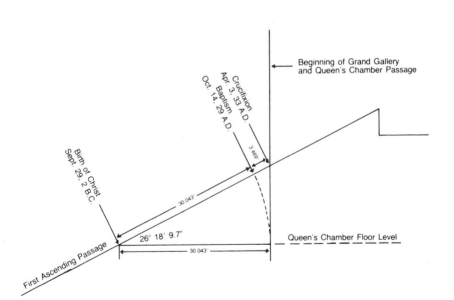

FIGURE 17

78

beautiful, perfectly hewn and polished lintels which topped the Sarsen Circle at Stonehenge had a vertical thickness of 28.4 inches.)

Could it be that the architect of the two greatest wonders of the world has left for us his autograph?

Notice in Figure 15 the last seven numerals in the decimal places of the length of the King's Chamber. The number 3168 is followed by the number 792. The random chance that this would occur is astronomical in probability.

This magnificently unique angle has been called, by some students of the Pyramid, the "Christ Angle" because it also bears, by its proportions, the relationship of the time between his birth, his baptism and his death. Considering one Pyramid inch to represent one year, the triangle reveals these remarkable dates:[4]

Right triangles of differing dimensions can be constructed, all bearing the same angle of 26° 18′ 9.7″. I constructed 160 such triangles, using random numbers, and numbers relating to the Creator, assigning to each triangle one number, either as the height, base or hypotenuse. When a random number was used, the other two sides of the triangle would produce numbers with no apparent significance. However, when numbers relating to the Creator were used, a definite pattern evolved—a pattern so remarkable I could hardly contain my excitement.

The name of the Creator, Jehovah (or Yahweh, as some call him), is really the "Unpronounceable Name." It was considered too sacred to pronounce, so the Hebrews spelled it with no vowel pointings, יהוה, rendering it unpronounceable. The numerical value is 26.

First, let's draw a right triangle whose angle is 26° 18′ 9.7″, and assign the number 26 to the base dimension. The height of the triangle will be 12.85 units. The number 1285 is the gematria for "The Holy City Jerusalem" η αγια πολις 'Ιερουσαλημ.

---

[4] The historical and astronomical evidence for these dates are included in Appendix II, which please see.

THE MAGNIFICENT NUMBERS

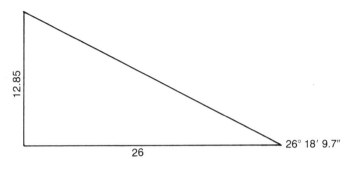

26 — Jehovah, יהוה
1285 — The Holy City Jerusalem,
η αγια πολις Ἰερουσαλημ

Next, draw another right triangle, using the same angle, and assign the number 26 to the hypotenuse. The height of the triangle will be 11.52, which is the gematria for ''The Kingdom of God,'' την βασιλειαν Θεου.

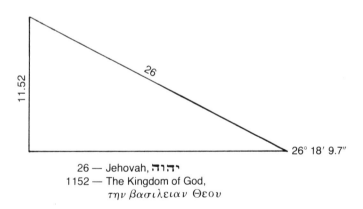

26 — Jehovah, יהוה
1152 — The Kingdom of God,
την βασιλειαν Θεου

God's typical kingdom was indeed in Jerusalem, but his glorious antitypical kingdom will be ''The Kingdom of God'' for which Jesus taught us to pray, *''Thy Kingdom come, thy will be done on earth as it is in heaven.''* (Matthew 6:10)

Draw a third triangle and this time assign the number 26 to the height. The hypotenuse will be 58.7 units. The gematria for God of Israel, אלהי ישר אל, is 587.

26 — Jehovah, יהוה
587 — God of Israel, אלהי ישר אל

The Pyramid passage angle unmistakably bears the number of its divine architect. Whether we assign the number 26 to the base, the height, or the hypotenuse of the triangle, the proportion bears important significance. It appears not to be by coincidence, but by the intelligent design of the architect. He has indeed left for us his autograph.

The only item of "furniture" in the entire Pyramid is the granite box in the King's Chamber. It was undoubtedly carved from a solid block of granite and lowered into the King's Chamber before the ceiling had been placed. This logical assumption is made on the basis of the obvious fact that the box is all of one piece, and the passages leading to this chamber are too small to permit it having been transported through them. This large, open, lidless granite box is called, by students of the Pyramid, the coffer, because of the suggestion by John Taylor that it was meant by the architect to serve as a "Standard Capacity Measure" for all nations of earth. Professor Smyth agreed with Taylor and showed that the capacity of the coffer, 71,250 cubic Pyramid inches, relates to the mean density of the earth in such a way as to provide a standard for weights and measures—

standards surprisingly close to the old Saxon weights and measures used in ancient Britain.

The calculation is done like this: the mean density of the earth is 5.7 times heavier than an equal mass of pure water at a temperature of 68°F, and a barometric pressure of 30 Pyramid inches. The interior of the coffer can hold 71,250 cubic Pyramid inches of such pure water. Therefore, a solid block of material, having the same density as the mean density of the earth, would need to be 5.7 times smaller in cubic capacity than the capacity of the coffer to be equal in weight to the weight of the water in the coffer.

The weight of the water in the coffer, or the weight of the hypothetical solid block, is the Great Pyramid's standard weight-measure, and has been called the Pyramid ton. By dividing one Pyramid ton by 2500 the result is the Pyramid pound—a weight remarkably similar to the old Saxon pound.

Just as the Pyramid inch is very nearly identical to the old Saxon inch, so the Pyramid pound suggests a connection with the ancient culture of Britain.

Today the metric system has been forced upon us as an attempt to unite the peoples and nations of the world with a universal standard. I was interested to note that the eminent Pyramidologist, Morton Edgar, suggested that the standards of weights and measures of the Great Pyramid will one day be the universal system of metrology.[5]

> In the future, not now far distant we believe, when the teaching of the Lord's Stone Witness in Egypt is more widely known and appreciated, and probably still more accurately interpreted, the earth-commensurable standards of linear measure, capacity measure, and weight measure which it presents, will be adopted by the whole human race, that all men may understand one another, speaking the same metrological language.

---

[5] Morton Edgar, *The Great Pyramid, its Scientific Features,* MacClure, MacDonald & Co., Glasgow, 1924, p. 134.

Notice in Figure 15 the number used to identify the length of the King's Chamber—412.13168792 Pyramid inches. Move the decimal point one place to the left and it becomes 41.213168792 Pyramid inches, which is the exterior height of the coffer. (And again we find the number value for Lord Jesus Christ, Κυριος 'Ιησους Χριστος, 3168, and the earth number, 792, in the numerals of the decimal.) This relationship of the coffer to the King's Chamber reveals the existence of a fore-ordained plan of the architect—the coffer was made for the King's Chamber; the King's Chamber was made for the coffer.

As we have shown, the Pyramid was constructed on the basis of the royal cubit; this being shown by the width of both the King's Chamber and the Queen's Chamber. It is interesting to note the correspondencies that exist between the royal cubit and the megalithic mile, using the coffer dimensions.

At Stonehenge, the distance from the center of the Sarsen Circle to the base of the Heel Stone is 256 British feet. It is on the basis of this measurement that Stonehenge reveals earth's distance to the sun as we have shown. When the 256 feet are converted to royal cubits, the distance is stated as 148.8 royal cubits. This number, 1488, appears again when we give the perimeter of the coffer in megalithic miles—.001488 MMi.

This interchange between royal cubits and megalithic miles occurs again with the coffer's relation to the Sarsen Circle. The diameter of the inner face of the Sarsen Circle is 56.6 royal cubits, and the floor diagonal of the coffer is .000566 MMi.

There is substantial evidence, however, that the coffer is much more than a standard capacity measure, or that it corresponds to other units in ancient metrology.

The prophet Isaiah spoke of the Great Pyramid as being a "witness" in the land of Egypt. A witness of what? A witness to whom? This mysterious empty, lidless granite box in the King's Chamber is a witness of the greatest event in the history of humanity.

Although the box has been made to appear to be a sarcophagus, for the entombment of a monarch, its witness, on the contrary is that of the resurrection of Jesus Christ. This is more than a mere assumption, it is the result of the piecing together of the puzzle and finding the beautiful picture that emerges.

When Caliph Al Mamoun first saw the coffer in A.D. 820, he described it as an "empty, lidless, stone chest." In all the records of the Pyramid, both ancient and modern, the coffer has, with one consent, been spoken of in this way. It has the *appearance* of a sarcophagus, but every evidence that it was never so used. Thus it has been reasoned, by earnest students of the Pyramid, that by its openness (no lid), and its emptiness (no mummy), it symbolizes a resurrection—the resurrection of Jesus. Is there more evidence that can be found to support this reasonable hypothesis? I believe there is.

I listed the numbers that define the dimensions of the coffer, using the linear units described in chapter 3. Then I compared with these a list of 100 4-digit random numbers to see how many would correspond. From my list of 100 random numbers, 8 were found to correspond to the numbers which define the dimensions of the coffer. Then I used a list of 100 numbers which are the gematria for the names and titles of Jesus, and phrases relating to his resurrection. There were 39 corresponding numbers, plus 18 duplicates. The evidence was overwhelming; the coffer does indeed relate to the resurrection of Jesus.

The numbers which confirm this beautiful relationship are listed below. Those who are familiar with the Bible will recognize the names and phrases as indeed pertaining to Jesus and his resurrection. I have cited the scripture references for those who desire to confirm their accuracy.

426 *Saviour* (Isaiah 19:20), מושיע
.0000426 of a sq. furlong - square of one side of interior of coffer.

1408 *Saviour*, σωτηρ
1.408 reeds - both (2) cubic diagonals of interior of coffer.
.001408 of a mile - one cubic diagonal of interior of coffer.

358 *Messiah* (Daniel 9:25), משיח
3.58 sq. great cubits - square of one end of exterior of coffer.

1480 *Christ (Messiah)*, Χριστος
.0001480 of a sq. furlong - square of inner surface of the coffer (not including a lid).

4126 *King of kings and Lord of lords* (Revelation 19:16)
Βασιλευς βασιλεων Κυριος κυριων
4.126 sq. yards - square of both (2) sides of interior of coffer.
41.26 British inches - height of exterior of coffer.

197 *Immanuel* (Isaiah 7:14), עמנו אל
.00197 of a furlong - diagonals (4) of both ends of interior of coffer.

888 *Jesus*, Ιησους
8880 *Behold, a virgin shall conceive and bear a son, and shall call his name Emmanuel, which being interpreted is, God with us.* (Matthew 1:23), ιδου η παρθενος εν γαστρι εξει και τεξεται υιον και καλεσουσν ονομα αυτου Εμμανουηλ ο εστιν μεθερμηνευομενον μεθ ημων Θεος
888 *Salvation of our God* (Isaiah 52:10), ישועת אלהינו
8.88 yards - perimeter of both (2) ends of exterior of coffer.
8.88 sq. Sumerian cubits - square of bottom of exterior of coffer.

2998 *Behold, a virgin shall conceive and bear a son* (Matthew 1:23)
ιδου η παρθενος εν γαστρι εξει και τεξεται υιον
2.998 MY - diagonal of bottom of exterior of coffer.

1666 *The only begotten Son* (John 3:16), τον υιον τον μονογενη
.1666 of a yard - thickness of sides of coffer.

1615 *Lamb of God* (John 1:36), αμνος του θεου
16.15 Sumerian cubits - perimeter of both (2) ends of exterior of coffer.

2197 *Jesus of Nazareth* (John 19:19), Ιησους ο Ναζωραιος
.02197 of a furlong - diagonals (4) of both ends of interior of coffer.

1333 *The child Jesus* (Luke 2:27), το παιδιον Ιησουν
13.33 feet - perimeter of one end of exterior of coffer.
1.333 MY - diagonal of one end of exterior of coffer.

THE MAGNIFICENT NUMBERS

4440 *The Lord Christ* (Colossians 3:24), τω κυριω Χριστω
4.44 yards - perimeter of one end of exterior of coffer.

1776 *Lord of the sabbath* (Mark 2:28), κυριος σαββατου
17.76 sq. Sumerian cubits - twice the square of the bottom of exterior of coffer (top and bottom).

649 *The Good Shepherd* (John 10:11), ο καλος ποιμην
6.49 feet - length of interior of coffer.

1111 *My Name* (Revelation 2:13), το ονομα μου
1111 *Name of the Son* (I John 5:13), ονομα υιου
111 *Wonderful* (Isaiah 9:6) , אלפ
11.1 sq. feet - square of one end of exterior of coffer.
.000111 of a sq. furlong - twice the square of the bottom of the exterior of coffer (top and bottom).
11.11 sq. sacred cubits - twice the square of the bottom of exterior of coffer (top and bottom).

1999 *Name of Jesus* (Acts 5:40), ονοματι του Ιησου
1999 *I am the Son of God* (John 10:36), υιος του Θεου ειμι
1.999 royal cubits - height of exterior of coffer.

2999 *Thou art the Son of God* (Mark 3:11), οτι συ ει ο υιος του Θεου
2.999 sq. MY - square of both (2) ends of exterior of coffer.
2.999 MY - diagonal of bottom of exterior of coffer.

3440 *The Light of the world* (John 8:12), το φως του κοσμου
3.44 feet - height of exterior of coffer.

281 *Lamb* (Revelation 21:23), αρνιον
.000000000281 of a cubic mile - inside capacity of coffer.

2442 *The Son of God* (Galatians 2:20), τη υιου του Θεου
2442 *Jesus, the name given by the angel* (Luke 2:21)
    Ιησους το κληθεν υπο αγγελου
244.2 British inches - perimeter of both (2) ends of interior of coffer.

5550 *Our Lord and his Christ* (Revelation 11:15)
κυριου ημων και του Χριστου αυτου
.0000555 of a square furlong - square of the bottom of exterior of coffer.

5.55 sacred cubits - combined height, width and length of interior of coffer.

5.55 sq. sacred cubits - square of bottom of exterior of coffer.

340 *Branch* (Isaiah 11:1) נצר
3.40 sacred cubits - diagonal of one side of interior of coffer.

1164 *Son of God* υιος Θεου
11.64 remens - combined height, width and length of exterior of coffer.

4216 *Christ, the Son of the blessed* (Mark 14:61)
Χριστος υιος του ευλογητου
4.216 royal cubits - diagonal of both (2) ends of interior of coffer.

222 *Nazarene* (Luke 4:34) Ναζαρηνε
22.2 sq. feet - square of both (2) ends of exterior of coffer.

876 *Prince of Peace* (Isaiah 9:6) שר שלום
8.76 sq. yards - square of interior surface of coffer (including top).

1221 *Holy Master* (Revelation 6:10) δεσποτης ο αγιος
122.1 British inches - perimeter of one end of interior of coffer.

1330 *Christ* Χριστου
133 *He is risen* (Matthew 28:6)
.00000133 of a sq. mile - square of both (2) sides of interior of coffer.

963 *Resurrection* αναστασις
.963 reeds - perimeter of end of interior of coffer.

2266 *The Resurrection* (Acts 4:33) της αναστασεως
22.66 Sumerian cubits - perimeter of both (2) sides of interior of coffer.

1544 *Resurrection of Him* (Matthew 27:53) εγερσιν αυτου
1.544 reeds - both diagonals of bottom of exterior of coffer.

.001544 of a mile - diagonal of bottom of exterior of coffer.

THE MAGNIFICENT NUMBERS

1997 *He is risen; he is not here* (Mark 16:6) ηγερθη ουκ εστιν ωδε
19.97 Sumerian cubits - diagonals of both (4) sides of exterior of
coffer.

2058 *He is not here, but is risen* (Luke 24:6) ουκ εστιν ωδε αλλ ηγερθη
2.058 sq. great cubits - square of end of exterior of coffer.

1832 *And the third day rise again* (Luke 24:7)
και τη τριτη ημερα αναστηναι
1832 sq. Pyramid inches - square of both (2) ends of interior of coffer.

4255 *Firstborn from the dead* (Revelation 1:15)
ο πρωτοτοκος των νεκρων
4.255 great cubits - length of exterior of coffer.

7881 *In him was life, and the life was the light of men* (John 1:4)
εν αυτω ζωη ην και η ζωη ην φως των ανθρωπων
7.881 MY - perimeter of floor of exterior of coffer.

5494 *In Christ shall all be made alive* (I Corinthians 15:22)
εν τω Χριστω παντες ξωοποιηθησονται
5.494 yards - both (2) diagonals of side of exterior of coffer.

The above list demonstrates beyond reasonable doubt that the
coffer symbolizes the resurrection of Jesus. It appears to be a
tomb, but one which does not hold death. For two thousand
years it reposed in eloquent silence, not the repository of death,
but a silent witness of the greatest event the human race has ever
known. The 16th day of the month Nisan, in the year A.D. 33,
the silent symbol became a glorious reality. The grieving
women who went early in the pre-dawn darkness to anoint the
body of Jesus, found only an empty tomb.

The Apostle Peter, reflecting on the importance of the event
exclaimed:

> *...whom God hath raised up, having loosed the pains of
> death: because it was not possible that he should be holden
> of it. For David speaketh concerning him "...Thou wilt
> not leave my soul in hell (hades, grave), neither wilt thou
> suffer thine Holy One to see corruption."*

Surely the coffer stands as a silent witness that Jesus indeed fulfilled the words spoken by King David, and quoted by Peter, for the gematria of the prophecy, $ουκ$ $εγκαταλειψεις$ $την$ $ψυχην$ $μου$ $εις$ $αδην$ $ουδε$ $δωσεις$ $τον$ $οσιον$ $σου$ $ιδειν$ $διαφθοραν$ has the numerical value of 8696. There are 8,696 square MY in the surface area of the interior of the coffer. Its entire empty interior speaks to us and proclaims *"Thou wilt not leave my soul in hell, neither wilt thou suffer thine Holy One to see corruption."*

The coffer—what a remarkable box—nothing short of fantastic! For four thousand years it held its precious secret. Only within the present century has its beautiful message been revealed. The coffer, by its dimensions, its construction, and its placement in the Great Pyramid, tells the world that there is indeed a resurrection of the dead.

While studying the geometry of that lonely ageless granite box, one number particularly called out for my attention—the number 2861 [6]—a magnificent number indeed. This beautiful number not only tells of the resurrection of Jesus, but it touches the lives of every one of us. It is a promise to us of life.

The Great Pyramid, as originally constructed, stood as a jewel in the desert, dazzling in the noonday sun. It was, however, from the beginning, without a topstone. The missing topstone was not the only seeming deficiency of the structure. To the observer, facing the front of the Pyramid (its northern face) the whole building appears to be somehow out of symmetry, giving it a look of imbalance and distortion. This illusion is due to the placement of the entrance—it is not in the center, but awkwardly to the left of center. Had the builder made a mistake? It is unthinkable that the master builder who designed that mathematical marvel could have made such an obvious error. Even if it were off center but a few inches we would wonder why, but it stands to the left of center an alarming and uncomfortable 286.1 Pyramid inches. A distance of nearly 24 feet.

Since all the interior passages and chambers were built in the

---

[6]Interior height of coffer = 2.861 feet
Square of one side of exterior of coffer = 2.861 sq. yards.

same vertical north-south plane as the entrance, it follows that the entire passage system of the monument is displaced eastward 286.1 Pyramid inches. The Belgian astronomer, Professor Charles Lagrange of the Royal Observatory, Brussels, named this displacement *Le Déplacement Charactéristique* (the Displacement Factor).

In the early years of this century the rubble and debris was cleared away from the base of the Pyramid, permitting accurate measurement of its base. The archaeologists who worked with the project were startled to find rectangular sockets beneath each of the four corners, and found that the building had been actually constructed shorter than its original design. The survey showed that the original full design had been that the base length (at socket level) should have been 9,131.05 Pyramid inches, but was actually constructed to measure 9,059.525 Pyramid inches. The base perimeter of the full design was found to be precisely 286.1 Pyramid inches larger than actually constructed. The deficiency of 286.1 Pyramid inches (the Displacement Factor) had been no mistake. It was careful, intelligent design!

This obvious deficiency in the construction of the monument would seem to suggest that the builder would, elsewhere in the structure, rectify or make it right. Since the Displacement Factor is a negative dimension of 286.1 Pyramid inches, an effective rectifying would require a plus dimension of 286.1 Pyramid inches. It would also seem logical that the rectifying of the displacement of the passage system would be found in the passage system, and the rectifying of the displacement of the exterior should be found somewhere in the exterior design; and so it is.

The rectification in the passage system was found to be in the height of the Grand Gallery. The two ascending passages (the First Ascending Passage and the Grand Gallery) share the same floor line; however, upon reaching the uppermost extremity of the First Ascending Passage and stepping into the spacious darkness of the Grand Gallery, we find the roof suddenly to be 286.1 Pyramid inches higher. This grand expansion of height is

A TOMB OR A TEMPLE?

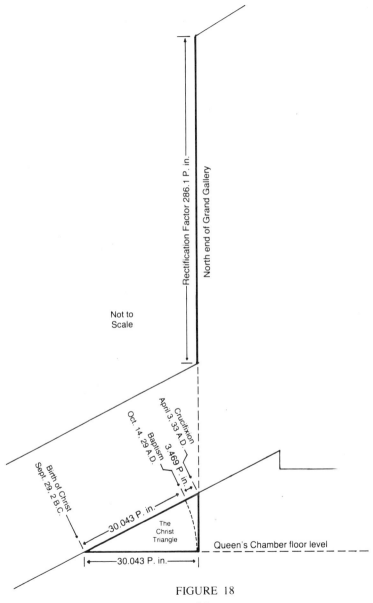

Rectification Factor 286.1 P. in.

North end of Grand Gallery

Not to Scale

Crucifixion
April 3, 33 A.D.

Baptism
Oct. 14, 29 A.D.

3.469 P. in.

Birth of Christ
Sept. 29, 2 B.C.

30.043 P. in.

The
Christ
Triangle

Queen's Chamber floor level

30.043 P. in.

FIGURE 18

directly above the Christ Triangle (see illustration, page 78). It was found to be a factor equal in dimension but opposite in function to the Displacement Factor; therefore it has been named the Rectification Factor.

That this Rectification Factor appears directly over the geometric illustration of the death and resurrection of Jesus, in A.D. 33, provides the fitting illustration of the value of his sacrificed life—it rectifies that which had been displaced by Adamic sin. The Apostle Paul expressed it thus:

For since by man (Adam) came death, by man (Jesus) came also the resurrection of the dead.'' (I Corinthians 15:21)

The Rectification Factor of the Great Pyramid reveals that the mighty power of the resurrected Jesus is the one great and only power adequate to rectify dying mankind and bring them to ultimate restitution. The Rectification Factor as found in the exterior design serves to verify and amplify this truth.

This beautiful white Pyramid was left without its crowning topstone. The topstone of a pyramid is the only stone in the structure which is itself a perfect pyramid, thus the topstone serves as a model for the whole building. The topstone for the Great Pyramid would have been enormous in size. Each side would have a length of 572.2 Pyramid inches (2 times the Rectification Factor). This is due to the displacement of the base of the structure from its original full design. Thus the 286.1 Pyramid inches by which the topstone would overhang exactly rectifies the 286.1 Pyramid inches in the displacement of the base of the monument. The base perimeter of the topstone would be 2288.8 Pyramid inches, which is precisely 8 times the Rectification Factor ($8 \times 286.1 = 2288.8$). The gematria for Christ the Lord, $X\rho\iota\sigma\tau\sigma\varsigma\ K\upsilon\rho\iota\sigma\varsigma$, is 2288, and 8 is the number used in the symbology of the Scriptures to represent the resurrection.

The base perimeter of the topstone is 111 royal cubits. What a beautiful number! It was the name given to Jesus in the prophecy of Isaiah 9:6 *"His name shall be called Wonderful..."* פלא,

111. The base diagonals (2) of this massive stone would have been 111 remens. The base of the topstone thus proclaims the name of Jesus. And its height (30 feet) tells us that he was a perfect man—the exact equivalent of Adam.

The Displacement Factor, when stated in reeds is 2.260, which is the gematria for Son of Man, $o\,\upsilon\iota os\,\alpha\nu\theta\rho\omega\pi o\upsilon$. He referred to himself by this title because it was necessary that he be a man—a corresponding price for Adam—in order to redeem Adam's posterity.

That this colossal mass of rock—this perfect topstone—should represent Jesus is referred to in both the Hebrew and Greek Scriptures.

"The stone which the builders refused is become the headstone of the corner, this is the Lord's doing; it is marvellous in our eyes." Psalm 118:22, 23

"He shall bring forth the headstone thereof with shoutings, crying, Grace, grace unto it." Zechariah 4:7

"Be it known unto you all, and to all the people of Israel, that by the name of Jesus Christ of Nazareth, whom ye crucified, whom God raised from the dead, even by him doth this man stand here before you whole. This is the stone which was set at nought of you builders, which is become the head of the corner. Neither is there salvation in any other: for there is none other name under heaven given among men, whereby we must be saved." Acts 4:10-12

"...and are built upon the foundation of the apostles and prophets, Jesus Christ himself being the chief corner stone." Ephesians 2:20

"Wherefore also it is contained in the scripture, Behold, I lay in Zion a chief corner stone, elect, precious: and he that believeth on him shall not be confounded. Unto you therefore which believe he is precious: but unto them which be disobedient, the stone which the builders disallowed, the same is made the head of the corner." I Peter 2:6, 7

THE MAGNIFICENT NUMBERS

> *"Therefore thus saith the Lord God, Behold, I lay in Zion
> for a foundation a stone, a tried stone, a precious corner-
> stone, a sure foundation."* Isaiah 28:16

The description of Jesus found in the prophecy of Isaiah 28:16
bears an interesting number value:

1460 *A precious cornerstone, a sure foundation.*
פנת יקרת מוסד מוס ד
14.6 sacred cubits - height of topstone
14.6 reeds - height of the combined 4 sides of topstone
.0146 of a mile - height of 2 sides of the topstone

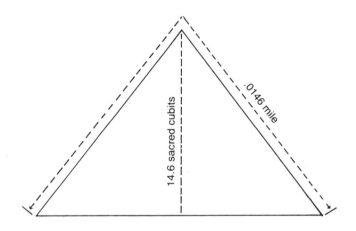

The scriptural record is quite clear: the topstone is indeed a
figure of Jesus. However, to further prove the correctness of the
concept, I tried the same mathematical game with the Pyramid
angle as I had done with the passage angle. Using the proportions of the topstone and the Pyramid angle of 51° 51′ 14.3″, I
constructed 100 triangles (mathematically), using random numbers, and the numbers that are the gematria of the names and
titles of Jesus. The triangles constructed with random numbers
produced dimensions with no apparent significance. However,
when I used numbers relating to Jesus for the base, the height, or

the hypotenuse, using the angle of 51 51′ 14.3″, the results appeared to have been the intentional design of the architect.

Construct a triangle representing the topstone. Assign 1164 units to the height. The hypotenuse will be 1480 units. The number 1164 is the gematria for Son of God, $υιος\,\Theta εου$, and 1480 is the gematria for Christ, $Χριστος$.

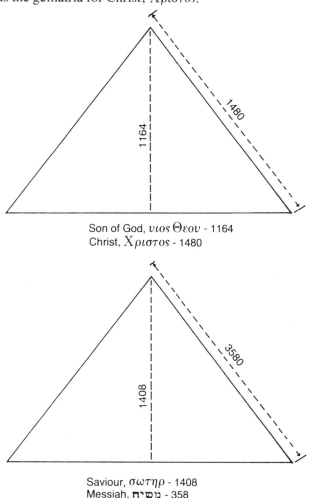

Son of God, $υιος\,\Theta εου$ - 1164
Christ, $Χριστος$ - 1480

Saviour, $σωτηρ$ - 1408
Messiah, נשׁיח - 358

Construct another triangle, and this time assign the number 1408 to the height. The hypotenuse will be 3580. The gematria for Saviour, $\sigma\omega\tau\eta\rho$, is 1408 and the number for Messiah, משיח, is 358.

Try another one, using Messiah, 358, as the height. Half the base (or the base of the right triangle) will be 281, which is the gematria for Lamb, $\alpha\varrho\nu\iota o\nu$, (Lamb of God).

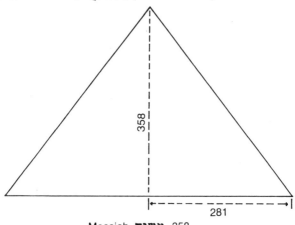

Messiah, משיח - 358
Lamb, $\alpha\varrho\nu\iota o\nu$ - 281

When John the baptist said "Behold the Lamb of God" he had reference to the purpose for which Jesus came to earth and became a man—that purpose being to give his life in sacrifice to redeem the human race. This act of giving his life in sacrifice had been pre-figured by the Jewish custom of killing a lamb at the time of Passover. The day that Jesus died on the cross on Calvary's hill, the Jews were killing their Passover lambs, thus he fulfilled the role of becoming the Lamb of God. It was at 3:00 in the afternoon, on Nisan 14 (April 3) A.D. 33 that he died on Calvary, the same hill where Abraham had offered his son Isaac. God had now offered his son Jesus. Calvary, the focal point for the salvation of the whole human race, was called in Hebrew, Golgotha, or the place of the skull. How appropriate to find that the topstone of the Pyramid, which so beautifully represents

Jesus, bears the name of the place of his sacrificed life. If the base of the topstone were assigned 186 units, the combined two sides would be 301 units. Calvary, $\kappa\rho\alpha\nu\iota\sigma\nu$, bears the number 301, while Golgotha, $\Gamma\sigma\lambda\gamma\sigma\theta\alpha$, has the number value of 186.

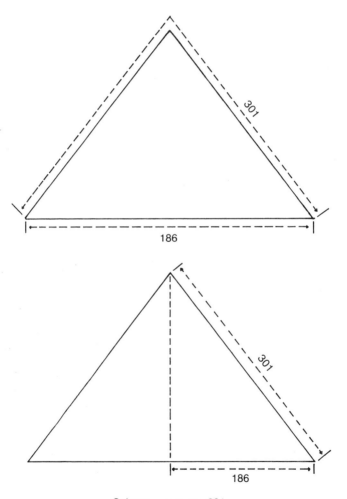

Calvary, $\kappa\rho\alpha\nu\iota\sigma\nu$ - 301
Golgotha, $\Gamma\sigma\lambda\gamma\sigma\theta\alpha$ - 186

THE MAGNIFICENT NUMBERS

In the light of the foregoing evidence, it seems not an unreasonable hypothesis that the Great Pyramid was indeed not a tomb, and was never designed for such a purpose, but rather, it was designed by the Almighty God as a witness and a testimony to his great plan of salvation for man, which was all embodied in the life, death and resurrection of Jesus. It was built two thousand years before Jesus came to earth to be man's redeemer. Time has progressed another two thousand years since that momentuous event, and the silent witness in the land of Egypt still stands. It still contains the empty granite box, proclaiming to all the world that death could not hold him — *"he is risen."*

By its Displacement and Rectification Factors, it tells the beautiful story of redemption, and the restoring to man of that which was lost through Adamic sin, *i.e.,* life.

I read recently that "Intellectuals have, and always will, debate the existence of God." I find that statement self-contradictory. It seems not particularly "intellectual" to ignore all the multitudinous evidences of an intelligent Creator.

That ageless, magnificent monument in the land of Egypt, though seemingly mute through the ages, now speaks to us of a loving and benevolent Creator who planned from the beginning for the ultimate good of his human family. It tells us, in stone, the same beautiful message that the Apostle John told us: *"God so loved the world that he gave his only begotten son."* (John 3:16)

Photo courtesy Todd Alexander, Pyramid Productions, Inc.

Photo courtesy Todd Alexander, Pyramid Productions, Inc.

The Great Pyramid stands as a silent sentinel as more than 1,500,000 mornings and evenings cast their shadows over the sands of the Nile delta.

Photo by Robert Alexander

Stonehenge stands lonely and forsaken in the morning mist. The Heelstone, seen through the sarsen arch 1-30 keeps its 4,000-year-old vigil over the monument.

6

What Is Stonehenge?

Theories about the origin and purpose of Stonehenge have been nearly as numerous as the centuries that have passed since its construction.

Many legends have come down to us through the ages, and the mystery of those ancient monoliths still haunts the minds of all who have pondered their origin. The very sight of Stonehenge, standing stark and silent on the lonely plain, arouses a feeling of mystery and the supernatural. That monument, unique in all the world, seems to defy human reasoning; so the imagination takes over where reason fails.

I cannot resist the impulse to tell of the legend of Merlin, the wizard, and his bargain with the devil to build Stonehenge. As the story goes, Merlin enlisted the aid of the devil in bringing from Ireland the stones with which to build the monument. The stones were, however, owned by an old woman, from whom the devil offered to purchase them. But the devil must, of course, be true to his stereotyped character, so he tricked her. He offered her as much money as she could count during the time it took him to lift and prepare them for transport. Being gullible, she eagerly accepted the bargain, thinking she would become rich. The devil handed her a purse filled with coins, but their values were rather difficult to count—four and a half pence, nine pence, thirteen and a half pence, etc. But as soon as she began to count, the devil told her to stop. He had completed bundling them and was ready to go. He picked them up, tossed them over his shoulder and flew off to Salisbury Plain. But even the poor devil is not without problems, for enroute to England, the rope with which the stones were tied began hurting him, and he attempted to lift them to his other shoulder. While executing this grand maneuver in mid-air one of the stones worked loose from the bundle and fell into the Avon. (The stone can still be seen today partly submerged in the Avon.) It was midnight when he arrived at Salisbury Plain—a most appropriate hour. And in the morning chill, just before dawn, the devil put the last stone into place. Standing back to admire his work, he said aloud, "No one will ever know how these stones came here, or from where."

Of such stuff are legends made. But legends have a strange effect upon people. Because of some unexplained and unexplored faculty of the human mind, it is easier to believe fiction than fact. But surely no one today would believe such a fabricated tale, or so it might seem, until we find the voluminous material which is being written and published today about the role of the devil and his demons in the building of Stonehenge. The basic story is the same; it is only dressed up in its Sunday clothes and made to appear credible. Today you can look in any encyclopedia and find the concept that the Druids built Stonehenge for purposes of their demon worship or for the purposes of human sacrifice. A popular concept today is that creatures from outer space built both Stonehenge and the Great Pyramid.

Why do such theories arise? And why are they accepted by the general public? Possibly because of the air of mystery that surrounds those incredible stone monuments, and the obvious super-human intelligence of the architect.

As early as 1793 James Douglas wrote that Stonehenge had been built long centuries before the Druids even came into existence, yet people today still believe it to have been built by the Druids.

In the early 1900s researchers began to suggest that Stonehenge was oriented to the rising of the summer sun.

In the 1950s Professor Gerald Hawkins, of Boston University,

an astronomer, spent much time at Stonehenge, observing the various sighting lines and collecting data which he took home and programmed into an IBM 7090 computer. That marvellous achievement of modern man, the computer, was necessary to unlock the secrets, to unravel the mystery, and to unveil the beauty of Stonehenge. Thanks to the brilliant work of Hawkins and his "machine," the mystery is still unfolding, and those silent stones begin to speak. The message that they tell not only takes us through 4,000 years of man's history, but far beyond, into the timeless forces of the universe, and into the future of man on this planet. The story of Stonehenge touches the lives of every one of us.

In 1880 Wm. Flinders Petrie wrote that the rising of the summer solstice sun over the Heel Stone was "mere coincidence."

As Hawkins began getting answers from his computer he knew that it was no "mere coincidence"—it was planned precision. He had not been prepared for such overwhelming evidence. He found that 12 of the significant Stonehenge alignments pointed to an extreme position of the sun, and 12 alignments pointed to an extreme position of the moon. [1]

Hawkins also discovered that the Aubrey Circle, with its 56 holes, served as a computer for the accurate prediction of eclipses. Many archaeologists doubted this concept, arguing that primitive people could in no way have arrived at such a

---

[1] Gerald S. Hawkins, *Stonehenge Decoded,* Dell Publishing Co., New York, p. 107.

sophisticated knowledge of astronomy. Hawkins was aware, however that 56 is a very important number to anyone interested in eclipses.

It is not easy to divide a circle into 56 equal sectors. So why this unusual number? Hawkins also noted the correspondence between the 29.5-day lunar month and the 30 stones of the Sarsen Circle with their 29 arches. Fully a decade after Hawkins' luminous work, Fred Hoyle suggested even a simpler method of operating the Stonehenge "computer." [2] To illustrate Hoyle's concept, we show a model of an earth-centered solar system, (Figure 19). The earth rotates counter-clockwise once each day and its axis of rotation is tilted toward the North Star. In this earth centered model, the sun and moon travel counter-clockwise around eliptic paths, the sun taking 365.242 days and

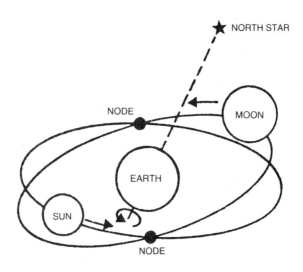

A simple earth-centered
model of our solar system.

FIGURE 19

[2] Fred Hoyle, *On Stonehenge,* W. F. Freeman and Company, 1977.

the moon taking 27.32 days. The paths are not on the same plane, one being slightly tilted with respect to the other. The points where their paths cross are called the *nodes* of the moon. These nodes move slowly clockwise, making a complete circuit in 18⅔ years, or 3 circuits in 56 years.

If a full moon occurs exactly on one of the nodes, the earth's shadow will fall across the moon—it will be a lunar eclipse. And because the earth's shadow is larger than the moon, the eclipse will be visible from anywhere on the night side of the earth. If a new moon occurs on one of the nodes, the moon's shadow will fall across part of the earth, and there will be a solar eclipse. Since the moon's shadow is smaller than the earth, the eclipse can be seen only in certain areas.

Did the builder of Stonehenge understand this eclipse cycle? The 56 holes of the Aubrey Circle attest that he did. By using four simple stones, the eclipse pattern can be simulated. The four stones represent the sun, the moon, and the two nodes. The procedure is like this: using the 56 holes of the Aubrey Circle, move the moon stone one hole counter-clockwise every morning and every evening. Move the sun stone one hole counter-clockwise every 6½ days (or once to every 13 moves of the moonstone). Move the node stones one hole clockwise three times a year (or once every 121 or 122 days).

These simulations of the movements of the sun and moon will gradually drift out of position, however, with observation of the new moon the necessary correction can be made. They can, however stay in proper relationship for at least a year. Thus the relative accuracy of the "computer" plus the actual sighting of the new moon when skies were clear enough to observe it, provided the means of predicting eclipses. But more importantly it showed the precision with which Stonehenge was related to the apparent movements of the sun and moon.

Stonehenge is, however, far more than a computer for predicting eclipses. Its relationship to the sun and moon and to the ages and history of man is without peer. Its circles and its stones are like a giant chronometer, ticking off the ages and actions of man.

The visitor to Stonehenge today still experiences a sense of mystery, a feeling of awe and wonderment as he walks in the shadows of those towering monoliths. The awesome antiquity of those timeless stones fall, like an avalanche, upon the awareness. It is as if a sixth sense were created within the mind—a sense of time and an identification with eternity.

In 1829 Godfrey Higgins suggested that the arrangement of the stones represented "astronomical cycles of antiquity." And indeed, astronomical cycles bear a relationship to the cycles of time and history.

A history of man has been preserved for us in the ancient Hebrew scriptures, as well as in the cuneiform records of the ancient kingdoms of Assyria, Egypt, Babylon and Persia. From these available records, a relative chronology of man can be extracted. Just as a computer supplied one of the keys with which to unlock the mysteries of Stonehenge, so the Bible proves to be another key to unlock its secrets and unveil its beauty. As the pieces of the puzzle begin to fit together, a beautiful picture emerges.

The chronology of the Bible is based on a cycle of 7,000 years. A *cycle* implies returning to a place from whence we started, or perhaps to a condition from whence we started.

The 56 holes of the Aubrey Circle at Stonehenge are, of course, evenly divisible by seven. It was this simple fact that aroused my curiosity to wonder if the 360° of the circle could, in some way, relate to the 7,000 years of man's history with which the Bible specifically deals. A circle has no beginning nor ending, and neither does eternity. However, one circuit of its circumference is a finite measure of eternity. Therefore, if the Aubrey Circle were to represent a period of 7,000 years relative to man's history as recorded in the Bible, it would be a simple matter to compute any given date around one complete circuit of its circumference (scale: 1 year = .0514285°).

Beginning with this simple hypothesis, considering the Aubrey Circle as a "date line," I was stunned with profound

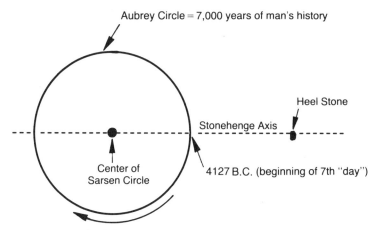

Aubrey Circle = 7,000 years of man's history

Heel Stone

Stonehenge Axis

Center of
Sarsen Circle

4127 B.C. (beginning of 7th "day")

amazement to find that the sun and moon alignments—every one of them—crossed the "date line" at significant dates in the history of man—dates that bore a relationship between man and his Creator. Not only did the sun and moon alignments tell the history of man, the stones of both the Bluestone Circle and Bluestone Horseshoe likewise revealed the chronology of the whole history of man's relationship with God.[3]

Professor Hawkins was so amazed at the multiplicity of sun and moon alignments at Stonehenge that he computed the probabilities. He found it to be ten million to one that those alignments could not have been by coincidence.

The alignment with which most people are acquainted is the azimuth of sunrise at the summer solstice, which appears to rise above the Heel Stone. As we have shown, this azimuth is 51° 51′ from north, and corresponds in such a beautiful way with the famous Pyramid angle, which is also 51° 51′.

The azimuth of the equinox moon at Stonehenge bears a similarly striking correspondence to the Great Pyramid.

The equinox is the mid-point between the two extremes of the sun, when night and day are of equal length. The equinox moon

---

[3] These dates and events are listed in detail in *Stonehenge...a closer look,* (Bonnie Gaunt), Crown Publishing Co., New York, chapters 2, 4 and 5.

is the full moon nearest the equinox.

But the moon has two maxima. It does not always cross the halfway point of its north-south swingings at the celestial equator. Because of these orbit plane motions, the full moon at the equinox can be anywhere from 5.14° north to 5.15° south of declination 0°. Thus the equinoctial swing is 10.30°. Because of this, several alignments of the equinox moon were found by Hawkins at Stonehenge. One of these was the alignment of Station Stone 94 to the Heel Stone.

The Heel Stone is of paramount importance to the astronomical significance of Stonehenge. Using the Heel Stone for finding the azimuth of the rising of the equinox moon (Passover moon) reveals an astonishing fact. If this alignment were moved to the center of the monument (a line drawn through the center that would parallel the 94-Heel Stone alignment) it becomes the only alignment in the whole structure to pass through *both* the Sarsen Center and the Aubrey Center. The apparent displacement of the Aubrey Center is thus cancelled by this one alignment, (similar to the rectifying of the Displacement Factor in the Great Pyramid). But the points at which this unique alignment intersect the Aubrey Circle (the date line) are startling!

The two date points at which this alignment interests the Aubrey Circle are the spring of 3473 B.C. and the spring of A.D. 33. On April 3, 33 A.D., Jesus hung upon a lonely cross atop Golgotha's hill. April 3 of that year was Israel's Passover. At 3:00 in the afternoon the Passover lambs were being slain. At 3:00 in the afternoon the Lamb of God died on the cross. At 3:06 Greenwich time (Stonehenge time) the moon eclipsed. An eclipse can only occur when the moon is full, and Passover is always observed when the equinox moon is full. As the moon rose over Jerusalem that awful night, it was still eclipsed for seventeen minutes.

The architect of Stonehenge has monumentalized in stone, for all time, and for all to see, the importance of the death of Jesus, the date of the event, and its occurrence on the afternoon of Passover (Equinox) moonrise!

108

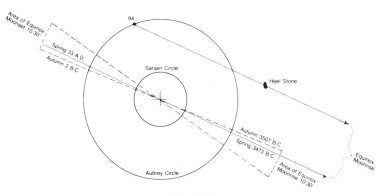

FIGURE 20

In Figure 17 we showed the remarkable "Christ Angle" in the Great Pyramid. The topmost point of this angle is the date point of April 3, 33 A.D. We have also shown (Figure 10) the relationship of the azimuth of summer sunrise at Stonehenge to the Pyramid angle. Now, let's fit the Pyramid angle into the sunrise angle at Stonehenge, thus giving the two monuments their actual size relationship.

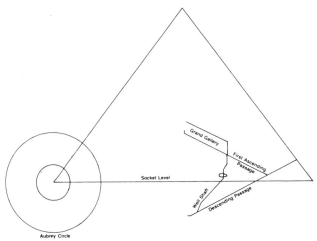

FIGURE 21

109

With the socket level of the Great Pyramid thus lined up with the summer solstice sunrise, trace up the First Ascending Passage to the point of intersection which marks the year A.D. 33 and draw a line parallel to the socket level. This line will intersect the Aubrey Circle at exactly the date A.D. 33. This forms a 33° angle with the Passover moonrise alignment. Such a precise correspondence between these two stone structures seems not possible to have been coincidence.

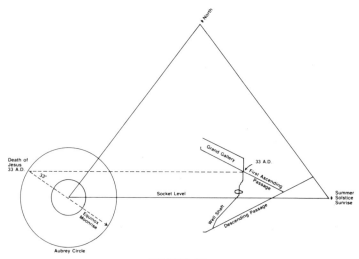

FIGURE 22

The architect of both monuments not only knew the angle of sunrise to north at latitute 51.17° on that remote plain in southern Britain, but he also knew the exact date of the greatest event in the history of man—the date of the death of man's Redeemer. This event was monumentalized in stone nearly 2,000 years before it happened. How could the architect have been other than the Creator Himself!

The evidences of a divine architect are everywhere to be found at Stonehenge. The magnificent numbers speak loudly and repeatedly of man's Redeemer. As if we might fail to note their importance, they have been repeated over and over again until the redundancy overwhelms us.

3168 - Lord Jesus Christ, $K\nu\rho\iota os\ \textrm{'}I\eta\sigma o\nu s\ X\rho\iota\sigma\tau os$
316.8 feet - mean circumference of Sarsen Circle
316.8 feet - perimeter of a square drawn on Bluestone Circle
316.8 yards - circumference of inner face of Inner Bank
3168 inches - long side of Station Stone Rectangle

888 - Jesus, $\textrm{'}I\eta\sigma o\nu s$
888 sq. yards - area of mean of Sarsen Circle
.00888 of a sq. furlong - area of a square of same perimeter as
        Bluestone Circle
.0888 of an acre - area of a square of same perimeter as Bluestone
        Circle

55 - Lord (Adon), אדן
.0055 of a MMi - diameter of Bluestone Circle

296 - Only Begotten, $\mu o\nu o\gamma\varepsilon\nu\eta$
2960 - Son of Man, $o\ \nu\iota os\ \alpha\nu\theta\rho\omega\pi o\nu$
2960 sq. royal cubits - area of outer face of Sarsen Circle

1164 - Son of God, $\nu\iota os\ \theta\varepsilon o\nu$
116.4 MY - mean circumference of Sarsen Circle
116.4 MY - perimeter of a square drawn on Bluestone Circle

2999 - Thou art the Son of God, $o\tau\iota\ \sigma\nu\ \varepsilon\iota\ o\ \nu\iota o\varsigma\ \Theta\varepsilon o\nu$
29.99 reeds - mean circumference of Sarsen Circle

2760 - Son of the Most High, $\nu\iota os\ \nu\psi\iota\sigma\tau o\nu$
27.6 yards - one side of a square of same perimeter as outer face of
        Sarsen Circle
276 remens - diameter of outer face of Inner Bank

THE MAGNIFICENT NUMBERS

1408 - Saviour, σωτηρ
140.8 yards - perimeter of a square drawn on outer face of Sarsen
      Circle

1777 - Jesus of Nazareth, Ιησους ο Ναζωραιος
177.7 royal cubits - circumference of inner face of Sarsen Circle
.01777 of a MMi - distance from Sarsen center to base of Heel Stone

1239 - Nazarene, Ναζωραιος
1239 sq. yards - area of a square drawn on outer face of Sarsen Circle

222 - Nazarene, Ναζαρηνε
.00222 of a sq. furlong - area of a square of same perimeter as
      Bluestone Horseshoe
.0222 of an acre - area of a square of same perimeter as Bluestone
      Horseshoe

358 - Messiah (Dan. 9), משיח
358 - The Arm of Jehovah (Isa. 53:1),
35.8 MY - diameter of inner face of Sarsen Circle

2182 - I am the Way, the Truth and the Life,
    εγω ειμι η οδος και η αληθεια και η ζωη
.02182 of a furlong - radius of Aubrey Circle
.2182 of a mile - perimeter of a square drawn on Aubrey Circle

352 - The Way, η οδος
3.52 feet - interval between Sarsen uprights
35.2 yards - diameter of outer face of Sarsen Circle
352 yards - circumference of outer face of Inner Bank

256 - Truth, αληθης
.0256 of a sq. furlong - area of a square drawn on outer face of Sarsen
      Circle
.256 of an acre - area of a square drawn on outer face of Sarsen Circle
256 feet - distance from Sarsen Center to base of Heel Stone
256 Sumerian cubits - perimeter of a square drawn on outer face of
      Sarsen Circle

264 - The Truth, $\eta \; \alpha \lambda \eta \theta \eta s$

26.4 yards - one side of a square of same perimeter as mean of Sarsen Circle

264 feet - one side of a square of same perimeter as outer face of Inner Bank

264 feet - long side of Station Stone Rectangle

26.4 yards - diameter of Bluestone Circle

1800 - Spiritual Rock (I Cor. 10:4), $\pi \nu \epsilon \nu \mu \alpha \tau \iota \kappa \eta s \; \pi \epsilon \tau \rho \alpha s$

180 great cubits - mean circumference of Sarsen Circle

180 great cubits - perimeter of a square drawn on Bluestone Circle

373 - Word (Logos), $\lambda o \gamma o s$

373 inches - one side of a square of same perimeter as Bluestone Horseshoe

138 - Branch (Jer. 23:5), נצר

138 sacred cubits - diagonal of Station Stone Rectangle

138 sacred cubits - diameter of Aubrey Circle

138 remens - radius of outer face of Inner Bank

138 royal cubits - one side of a square of same perimeter as inner face of Inner Bank

281 - Lamb, $\alpha \varrho \nu \iota o \nu$

28.1 MY - one side of a square of same perimeter as inner face of Sarsen Circle

.0000281 of a sq. mile - area of a square of same perimeter as inner face of Sarsen Circle

586 - Master, $o \; \delta \iota \delta \alpha \sigma \kappa \alpha \lambda o s$

58.6 royal cubits - diameter of mean of Sarsen Circle

115 - Rabbi, $\rho \alpha \beta \beta \iota$

115 feet - short side of Station Stone Rectangle

11.5 royal cubits - radius of Bluestone Horseshoe

185 - Rabbi, $o \rho \alpha \beta \beta \iota$
18.5 MY - radius of mean of Sarsen Circle
.00185 of a sq. mile - area of a square of same perimeter as Aubrey Circle
185 royal cubits - diameter of crest of Inner Bank
185 Sumerian cubits - circumference of inner face of Sarsen Circle

2580 - Bright and Morning Star (Rev. 22:6),
$\alpha \sigma \tau \eta \rho \ o \ \lambda \alpha \mu \pi \rho o s \ o \ \pi \rho \omega \iota \nu s$
258 feet - distance from Sarsen Center to center of Heel Stone

The Hebrew prophet Isaiah has recorded for us a prophecy concerning the birth of man's Redeemer, and his ultimate purpose in relation to man. Those who celebrate Christmas are familiar with the prophecy, for it is often quoted at that season of the year:

> *For unto us a child is born, unto us a son is given: and the government shall be upon His shoulder: and His name shall be called Wonderful, Counsellor, the Mighty God, the Everlasting Father, the Prince of Peace. Of the increase of His government and peace there shall be no end....''* (Isaiah 9:6, 7)

The names given to this child that was to be born signify his greatness and the scope of his work and authority. And, as we might suspect, each of the names is recorded in the magnificent numbers of Stonehenge.

111 - Wonderful, פלא
111 MY - diameter of inner face of Inner Bank

176 - Counsellor, יועץ
17.6 yards - radius of outer face of Sarsen Circle
.000176 of a sq. mile - area of Bluestone Circle

242 - Mighty God, **אל גבור**
242 reeds - distance from Sarsen Center to base of Heel Stone
242 sacred cubits - radius of mean of Sarsen Circle

87 - Everlasting Father, **אבי עד**
87 remens - diameter of outer face of Sarsen Circle
8.7 sq. reeds - area of a square of same perimeter as
               Bluestone Horseshoe
87 Sumerian cubits - radius of Aubrey Circle

876 - Prince of Peace, **שר שלום**
8760 sq. feet - area of outer face of Sarsen Circle
87.6 MY - distance from open end of Bluestone Horseshoe to center of
    Heel Stone

The titles "Mighty God" and "Everlasting Father" are easily confused with the concept of Jehovah. In the original Hebrew text the definite article (the) does not appear before these titles, as it does in the King James translation. The titles are descriptive of the work and authority of that one who came as a lowly babe, born in Bethlehem. Because he purchased the human race by redeeming them from the death-curse, he had the power and the authority to father them with everlasting life. How thrilling to find that this great work is recorded in number—recorded in stone. Those silent stones have kept their secret for 4,000 years. But during the interim a child indeed was born to fulfill the prophecy. And just as assuredly the government of the world will yet be upon his shoulder, and his name will indeed be called

> *"Wonderful, Counsellor,...*
> *Mighty God,...Everlasting Father,...*
> *Prince of Peace...."*

The Apostle John told of a love that surpasses all other love— the love of God for man. It was a love that caused him to give his only begotten son to be man's Redeemer:

115

*God so loved the world that He gave his only begotten son,
that whosoever believeth in him should not perish, but have
everlasting life.* (John 3:16)

Stonehenge, by its geometry, indeed tells of God's supreme
gift—the Redeemer, the Messiah.

The architect of that ancient stone wonder has not only
revealed the story of the redemption of man, but he left there,
for us, his autograph. The author of the plan of redemption, the
architect of Stonehenge, has placed his name in the geometry of
those stone circles—not once, but over and over again.

The beautiful prayer of King David in II Samuel 22:3, which
so clearly related to the geometry of Israel's temple (see page
57), also relates to the geometry of Stonehenge.

*The God of my Rock, he is my shield, and the horn of my
salvation, my high tower, and my refuge.*

352 - The God of my Rock, אלהי צורי
35.2 yards - diameter of outer face of Sarsen Circle
35.2 yards - circumference of outer face of Inner Bank
3.52 feet - interval between Sarsen uprights

172 - My Refuge, ומנוסי
172 great cubits - diameter of inner face of Inner Bank
(1.72 feet = 1 royal cubit)

1728 - The God of my rock, he is my shield and the horn of my
    salvation, my high tower and my refuge,
    אלהי צורי מגני וקרן ישעי משגבי ומנוסי
1,728 inches - radius of Aubrey Circle
.01728 of a MMi. - circumference of Bluestone Circle

The Creator is known by many names in the Bible. It is not by
coincidence that these names can be found in the geometry of
Stonehenge.

1822 - Almighty, $\pi\alpha\nu\tau\omega\kappa\rho\alpha\tau\omega\rho$

18,222 sq. great cubits - area of a square of same perimeter as inner face of Inner Bank

124 - Jehovah is my God, יהוה הוא אלהים

124 remens - radius of inner face of Inner Bank

74 - A great God, אל גדול

.074 of a furlong - radius of inner face of Sarsen Circle

.074 of a mile - perimeter of a square drawn on inner face of Sarsen Circle

100 - A great God is Jehovah, אל גדול יהוה

100 reeds - circumference of outer face of Inner Bank

100 sq. reeds - area of a square drawn on outer face of Sarsen Circle

86 - God (Elohim), אלהים

86 - The majesty of Jehovah, גאון יהוה

86 yards - distance from Sarsen Center to center of Heel Stone

86 great cubits - radius of inner face of Inner Bank

26 - Jehovah, יהוה

260 remens - circumference of mean of Sarsen Circle

371 - Jehovah-shammah, יהוה שמה

37.1 MY - diameter of mean of Sarsen Circle

276 - Jehovah-tsidkenu, יהוה צדקנו

27.6 yards - one side of a square of same perimeter as outer face of Sarsen Circle

276 remens - diameter of outer face of Inner Bank

242, Jehovah-jirah, יהוה יראה

24.2 sacred cubits - radius of mean of Sarsen Circle

24.2 reeds - distance from Sarsen Center to base of Heel Stone

2444 - The Lord your God (Acts 3:22), Κυριος ο Θεος υμων
.0002444 of a MMi. - interval between Sarsen uprights
244.4 Sumerian cubits - perimeter of a square drawn on mean of
    Sarsen Circle

222 - Jehovah God Most High (Gen. 14:22), יהוה אל עליון
222 - I am Jehovah your God (Ex. 6:7), כי אני יהוה אלהיכם
.00222 of a sq. furlong - area of a square of same perimeter as
    Bluestone Horseshoe
.0222 of an acre - area of a square of same perimeter as
    Bluestone Horseshoe
2220 sq. great cubits - area of a square of same perimeter as outer face
    of Sarsen Circle

3330 - God the saviour, Θεω τω σωτηρι
.333 reeds - interval between Sarsen uprights
333 yards - circumference of crest of Inner Bank

2664 - The Lord God is one Lord, κυριος Θεος κυριος εις εστιν
.0002664 of a sq. mile - area of inner face of Sarsen Circle

314 - Almighty, שדי
.000314 of a sq. MMi - area of Aubrey Circle
.000314 of a sq. mile - area of outer face of Sarsen Circle
31.4 reeds - circumference of outer face of Sarsen Circle

    The list is overwhelming. It satiates the senses and jams the
comprehension. If there had been two or perhaps three significant dimensions at Stonehenge, we could easily have pointed to
them and said, ''See, the Creator has left his number there.''
But twenty scrambles the thinking and shatters the awareness.
Why did the architect of Stonehenge leave his numbers there
with such obvious redundancy? Was it so we would recognize it
as being his handiwork? It hardly seems possible, in view of the
obvious fact that 4,000 years of its history have been shrouded in
mystery. Nor can we reason that its message failed of its

intended purpose. To do so would be to lose all faith in the One who planned for eternity, who knows the "end from the beginning." Its message—if indeed it is a divine message—cannot fail. Jehovah gave the firm assurance:

For my thoughts are not your thoughts, neither are your ways my ways, saith the Lord. For as the heavens are higher than the earth, so are my ways higher than your ways, and my thoughts than your thoughts. For as the rain cometh down, and the snow from heaven, and returneth not thither, but watereth the earth, and maketh it bring forth and bud, that it may give seed to the sower, and bread to the eater: so shall my word be that goeth forth out of my mouth: it shall not return unto me void, but it shall accomplish that which I please, and it shall prosper in the thing whereto I sent it. (Isaiah 55:8-11)

Thus it follows to a logical conclusion that if it is a divine message it will someday, in some way, be proclaimed. Perhaps the time is not far distant when the depth of the meaning of Stonehenge, and the purpose for which the Creator designed it, will indeed be unfolded, and the mysteries fully revealed.

Stonehenge not only tells us of the Creator, and his plan for the ultimate salvation of man, through the coming of the Messiah; it also tells us of the cosmos as it directly relates to man, *i.e.*, the earth, sun and moon. As the relationship of Stonehenge to these orbs unfolds, it becomes apparent that the architect was using an intricate pattern of numbers—magnificent numbers, if you please, for they are elements of the building blocks of creation. Stonehenge, by its geometry, becomes a microcosm of the universe.

All of the circles of Stonehenge bear a beautiful relationship to the earth, sun and moon. Let's start by noting the similarity of the Bluestone Circle to the earth and moon. The circumference of all three bear the same number, described by three different units, all of which are in the family of the British mile.

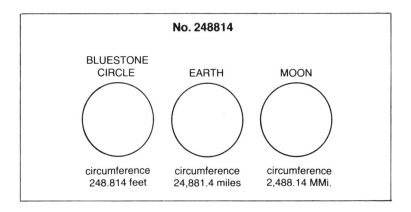

The numerical relationship would not exist without the British mile and the British foot units. And it is highly unlikely that these numerical relationships would have existed had the builder of Stonehenge not known the circumference of the earth. Did man 4,000 years ago possess such knowledge?

Eratosthenes of Alexandria (c. 276-194 B.C.) is considered the founder of geodesy because he is claimed to be the first man to measure the size of the earth. He had become aware of a unique phenomenon. At high noon at the summer solstice in the city of Syene, in Upper Egypt, the sun shone directly down a well, the sides of the well casting no shadow on the water below, *i.e.,* the sun was directly overhead. He observed that a vertical pole would likewise cast no shadow. Returning to Alexandria he noted that a vertical pole did indeed cast a shadow. These two observations, he reasoned, were evidence for a spherical earth. But they were much more. His measurements showed that the direction of the sunlight at Alexandria was at an angle of 360°/50 or 7.2°, thus he concluded that the central angle between Syene and Alexandria was 7.2°. He then attempted to obtain the distance from Syene to Alexandria. From this he could calculate the circumference of the earth. Surprisingly enough, his calculation was within 50 miles of present day figures.

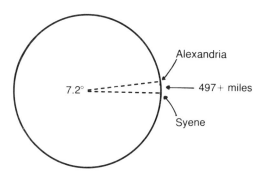

FIGURE 23

The next known attempt to determine the size of the earth was done by Poseidonius (c. 135-50 B.C.). He measured the distance between Rhodus and Alexandria by the length of time required for a boat to sail between them. He determined the central angle between Rhodus and Alexandria by astronomical observations. His calculation proved to be approximately 11% too large.

Nine hundred years later the Caliph Al Mamoun had measurements taken of an arc of the earth's circumference on the plateau of Zinjar, near Baghdad, using wooden measuring rods. His measurements were quite accurate, proving to be only about 3.6% too long.

In view of these attempts at measuring the earth, how did man 4,000 years ago have such accurate knowledge of geodesy to enable him to build into the circles of Stonhenge this precise relationship to the earth? Such a striking relationship would not likely have been by chance. However, if some are hesitant to rule out chance, may we look further at those 4,000 year old circles and their numerical relation to the cosmos. Following is a graphic outline of the evidence. I ask that the reader consider it in the time frame of 1973 B.C., and the knowledge of astronomy and earth science available to man in that remote age—man without the aid of telescopes, geo-physics, or computers.

Stonehenge Geometric Relationship
to Earth, Sun and Moon

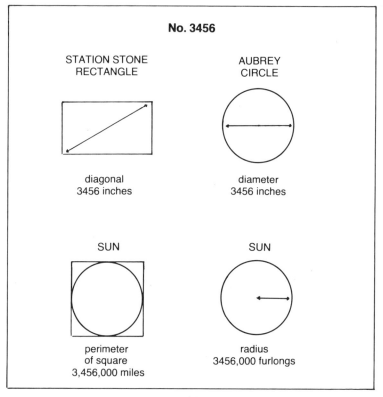

No. 3456

STATION STONE
RECTANGLE

diagonal
3456 inches

AUBREY
CIRCLE

diameter
3456 inches

SUN

perimeter
of square
3,456,000 miles

SUN

radius
3456,000 furlongs

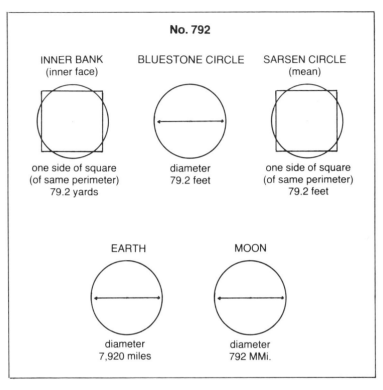

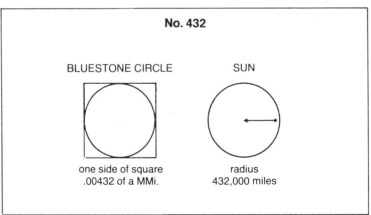

THE MAGNIFICENT NUMBERS

No. 69696

SARSEN CIRCLE
(mean)

area of square
(of same perimeter)
696.96 sq. yards

INNER BANK
(outer face)

area of square
(of same perimeter)
69,696 sq. feet

BLUESTONE CIRCLE

area of square
696.96 sq. yards

EARTH

radius
6,969,600 yards

No. 6336

SARSEN CIRCLE
(outer face)

radius
633.6 inches

EARTH

diameter
63,360 furlongs

WHAT IS STONEHENGE?

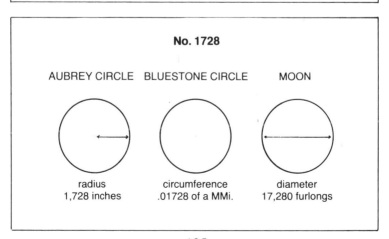

No. 396

BLUESTONE CIRCLE   BLUESTONE HORSESHOE

radius
39.6 feet

diameter
39.6 feet

EARTH

MOON

radius 3,960 miles

radius
396 MMi.

No. 1728

AUBREY CIRCLE   BLUESTONE CIRCLE   MOON

radius
1,728 inches

circumference
.01728 of a MMi.

diameter
17,280 furlongs

THE MAGNIFICENT NUMBERS

No. 3168

SARSEN CIRCLE
(mean)

BLUESTONE CIRCLE

INNER BANK
(outer face)

circumference
316.8 feet

perimeter of square
316.8 feet

one side of square
(of same perimeter)
3,168 inches

STATION STONE
RECTANGLE

INNER BANK
(inner face)

SUN

long side
3,168 inches

circumference
316.8 yards

diameter
316,800 MMi.

MOON

EARTH

EARTH

perimeter of square
3,168 MMi.

perimeter of square
31,680 miles

radius
31,680 furlongs

126

WHAT IS STONEHENGE?

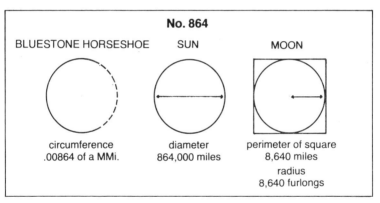

No. 12672

INNER BANK (outer face)	SARSEN CIRCLE (outer face)	SUN
circumference 12,672 inches	diameter 1,267.2 inches	perimeter of square 1,267,200 MMi.

No. 864

BLUESTONE HORSESHOE	SUN	MOON
circumference .00864 of a MMi.	diameter 864,000 miles	perimeter of square 8,640 miles radius 8,640 furlongs

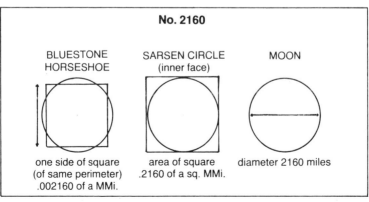

No. 2160

BLUESTONE HORSESHOE	SARSEN CIRCLE (inner face)	MOON
one side of square (of same perimeter) .002160 of a MMi.	area of square .2160 of a sq. MMi.	diameter 2160 miles

THE MAGNIFICENT NUMBERS

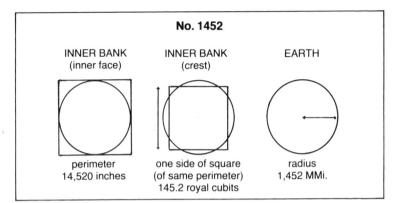

No. 1452

INNER BANK
(inner face)

INNER BANK
(crest)

EARTH

perimeter
14,520 inches

one side of square
(of same perimeter)
145.2 royal cubits

radius
1,452 MMi.

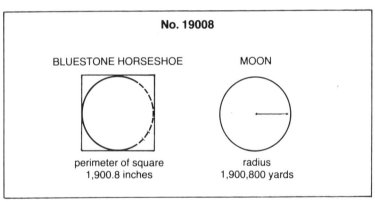

No. 19008

BLUESTONE HORSESHOE

MOON

perimeter of square
1,900.8 inches

radius
1,900,800 yards

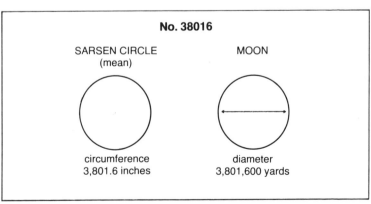

No. 38016

SARSEN CIRCLE
(mean)

MOON

circumference
3,801.6 inches

diameter
3,801,600 yards

WHAT IS STONEHENGE?

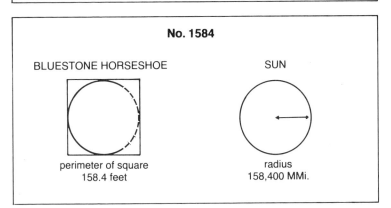

No. 2714336

AUBREY CIRCLE

one side of square
(of same perimeter)
2,714.336 inches

SUN

circumference
2,714,336 miles

No. 1584

BLUESTONE HORSESHOE

perimeter of square
158.4 feet

SUN

radius
158,400 MMi.

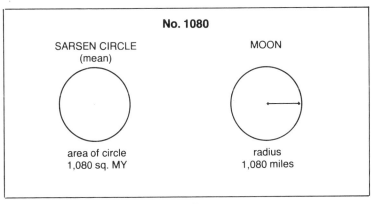

No. 1080

SARSEN CIRCLE
(mean)

area of circle
1,080 sq. MY

MOON

radius
1,080 miles

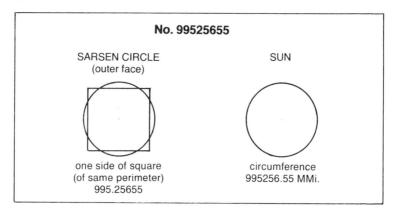

No. 99525655

SARSEN CIRCLE
(outer face)

SUN

one side of square
(of same perimeter)
995.25655

circumference
995256.55 MMi.

In the light of such overwhelming evidence, I do not hesitate to affirm my conviction that the architect of Stonehenge was none other than the architect of the earth, sun and moon—man's Creator!

His agent in all the works of creation was his son, the Lord Jesus Christ. This is clearly stated in John 1:3: *"All things were made by him; and without him was not anything made that was made."*

The number of his name, 3168, is one of the magnificent numbers of Stonehenge. The diagrams above show the beautiful relationship of this number to the cosmos. It defines the dimensions of the earth, sun and moon.

The circle and the square are fundamental opposites. It is mathematically impossible to square the circle because of the irrational nature of π.[4] Yet the Creator has shown over and over again a relationship between these two opposing concepts, not by squaring the circle, but by a circle and square of equal perimeters. The relationship of the Sarsen Circle to the Bluestone Circle is a beautiful illustration of this.

The defining of both by the same perimeter, 316.8 feet, illustrates his ultimate plan of reconciling man to himself through the

---

[4]To square the circle is to obtain a square whose area equals the area of the circle.

redeeming work of the Lord Jesus Christ (3168). It is an everlasting oneness between man and his Creator—a marriage of the circle and the square.

Perimeter of a square drawn on Bluestone Circle, 316.8 feet.
Circumference of Sarsen Circle, 316.8 feet.

The squaring of the circle is, however, found in the relationship of the earth and sun. The sun always represents the source of light and life, the Creator himself. Earth, on the other hand, pertains to man. The work of reconciling man to himself covers a period of 7,000 years, from the disobedience of Adam to the completion of the work of restitution at the end of earth's great millennium. How fitting therefore to find that the squaring of the circle can be found in the ratio of one sun to seven earths.

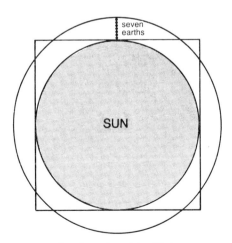

The Squaring of the Circle
(square and circle of equal area)

THE MAGNIFICENT NUMBERS

The geometry of the earth has always been the basis for our system of metrology, both ancient and modern. The relationship of the cosmos to Stonehenge gives another clue to its purpose. Just as the coffer in the Great Pyramid was found to be a standard capacity measure, so Stonehenge proves to be a standard for linear measure.

The perfectly shaped lintels which topped the Sarsen uprights had a mean length of 10.56 feet each. Thirty such stones formed the circle of 316.8 feet. Each of these lintels is, in fact, a 500th part of a mile. The width of the lintels, 3.4757485 feet, is 1/6,000,000 of the polar radius of the earth.[5] The great care that was taken in the cutting and shaping of these lintel stones reveals a careful concern for precision. Because of such precision they effectively serve as a standard for the British mile.

Did man, 4,000 years ago use the British mile? It is evident that he did.

The Station Stone Rectangle served as a similar standard. Its long side measured 264 feet, which is the 20th part of a mile. The builder of Stonehenge left for us a permanent repository for the mile unit. Any such standard that can endure through 4,000 years is indeed a monument, not only to metrology, but also to the wisdom and forsight of its builder.

The Sarsen Circle and the Inner Bank also serve as a standard for the mile unit. The outer face of the Sarsen Circle has a radius of 52.8 feet, which is the 100th part of the British mile. The outer face of the Inner Bank has a circumference of 1056 feet, which is the 5th part of a mile.

What about other units in ancient metrology? Are standards for these units to be found at Stonehenge?

Just as the long side of the Station Stone Rectangle served as a standard for the British mile, so it also serves as a standard for other units in the family of British metrology, *viz.*, the inch, the foot, the yard, and the furlong. It also is a standard for other

---

[5]The width of the lintels, like many other dimensions of Stonehenge and the Great Pyramid, is obtained by geometric proportions.

ancient units: the Egyptian remen, the Sumerian cubit, the great cubit, and the reed.

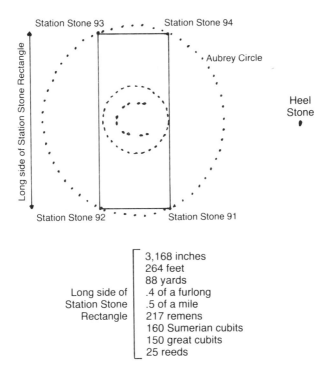

Long side of Station Stone Rectangle	3,168 inches
	264 feet
	88 yards
	.4 of a furlong
	.5 of a mile
	217 remens
	160 Sumerian cubits
	150 great cubits
	25 reeds

The beautiful curved lintels of the Sarsen Circle not only served as a repository for the standard for the British mile, but also for the great cubit and the reed. The mean length of each lintel is identical to the length of the reed—10.56 feet. Thus each lintel also measures 6 great cubits.

The linear units of ancient metrology are to be found in many other ways at Stonehenge. All of these are found in their relation to the British foot and mile. The list below shows the abundance of evidence that these units were known to the builder.

THE MAGNIFICENT NUMBERS

12 inches = 1 foot
12 Sumerian cubits - radius of Bluestone Horseshoe

36 inches = 1 yard
3600 sq. great cubits - area of square drawn on outer face of
     Sarsen Circle

7920 inches = 1 furlong
79.2 feet - one side of a square of same perimeter as mean of
     Sarsen Circle
79.2 feet - diameter of Bluestone Circle
79.2 yards - one side of a square of same perimeter as inner face of
     Inner Bank

63360 inches = 1 mile
633.6 inches - radius of outer face of Sarsen Circle

31680 inches = ½ mile
3168 inches - long side of Station Stone Rectangle
316.8 feet - circumference of mean of Sarsen Circle
316.8 feet - perimeter of a square drawn on Bluestone Circle
3168 inches - one side of a square of same perimeter as outer face of
     Inner Bank
316.8 yards - circumference of inner face of Inner Bank

15840 inches = ¼ mile
1584 feet - perimeter of a square drawn on Bluestone Horseshoe

12672 inches = 1/5 mile
126.72 inches = 1 reed
1267.2 inches - diameter of outer face of Sarsen Circle
12672 inches - circumference of outer face of Inner Bank

10560 inches = 1/6 mile
10.56 feet = 1 reed
105.60 yards - circumference of mean of Sarsen Circle
105.6 feet - diameter of outer face of Sarsen Circle
105.6 yards - perimeter of a square drawn on Bluestone Circle
1056 feet - circumference of outer face of Inner Bank

19.8 inches = 1 Sumerian cubit
19.8 feet - radius of Bluestone Horseshoe

172800 inches = 1 MMi.
1728 inches - radius of Aubrey Circle
.01728 of a MMi. - circumference of Bluestone Circle

660 feet = 1 furlong
6.60 yards - radius of Bluestone Horseshoe
.066 MMi. - circumference of inner face of Inner Bank

5280 feet = 1 mile
52.80 yards - perimeter of square drawn on Bluestone Horseshoe
52.80 feet - radius of outer face of Sarsen Circle
528.0 feet - both sides (2 × length) of Station Stone Rectangle

1.65 feet = 1 Sumerian cubit
.0165 MMi. - one side of a square of same perimeter as inner face of
        Inner Bank
1.65 acres - area of inner face of Inner Bank

1.72 feet = 1 royal cubit
172 yards - 2 × distance from Sarsen Center to center of Heel Stone
        (Stonehenge Axis)
172 great cubits - diameter of inner face of Inner Bank

1.76 feet = 1 great cubit
17.6 yards - radius of outer face of Sarsen Circle
176 royal cubits - diameter of inner face of Inner Bank

2.72 feet — 1 megalithic yard (MY)
.000272 of a sq. MMi. - area of a square of same perimeter as
        inner face of Inner Bank

14,400 feet = 1 megalithic mile (MMi.)
144 feet - radius of Aubrey Circle
.144 acres - area of a square of same perimeter as mean of
        Sarsen Circle
.144 acres - area of a square drawn on Bluestone Circle
1.44 furlongs - circumference of inner face of Inner Bank
144 Sumerian cubits - one side of a square of same perimeter as
        inner face of Inner Bank

135

2.727272 miles = 1 megalithic mile (MMi.)
272.72 remens - circumference of outer face of Sarsen Circle
27.272 reeds - diagonal of Station Stone Rectangle
27.272 reeds - diameter of Aubrey Circle

The standard for π has also been built into those magnificent stone circles. The outer face of the Sarsen Circle has a circumference of 31.4159 reeds, or 10 times π .

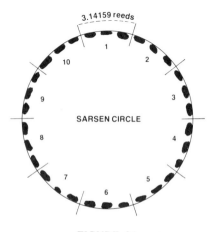

FIGURE 24

And, as if to emphasize the importance of that circle to the π value, and to the British mile, the area within its outer face is .000314159 of a sq. mile.

In light of all the evidence that has been brought to bear, some logical conclusions can be obtained. It has appeared evident that the Creator was the architect of Stonehenge; it also appears evident that Stonehenge was a repository for the standards of the units in ancient metrology, units which are based upon the dimensions of the earth. Therefore 1) these units were either known or in use at the time of the construction of Stonehenge; 2) these units had a common origin for they fit into one synergistic pattern, and the originators of them knew the dimensions of the earth; 3) these units could have been given to man by the Creator.

Other evidences of the antiquity of the British mile (and its family) can be found beyond Stonehenge.

The distance from Stonehenge to Silbury Hill is 86,400 feet, or 6 megalithic miles. From the center of Silbury Hill to the center of Avebury is exactly one mile (5280 feet). Avebury is a circular stone-and-earth-work which dates back to the era of the building of Stonehenge and Silbury Hill. The ancients who constructed these works evidently used these linear units.

Professor A. Thom has shown from surveys of the megalithic sites in Britain that their builders used these standard units of length. From these observations he discovered the addition of units which he termed the megalithic yard (2.72 feet), the megalithic rod (2½ MY), and the megalithic mile, (2.727272 miles, or 14,400 feet). John Michell has shown that the latter is identical to the ancient oriental pu-mile.[6]

Yes, Stonehenge is many things—a standard for linear units of measure, a prophetic time device, an astronomical observatory, a computer for the predicting of eclipses. But most of all, it is evidence for the existence of an intelligent Creator—a Creator who planned (and carried out that plan) for the ultimate good of his human family, through the redeeming work of Jesus Christ.

---

[6] John Michell, *Ancient Metrology*, Pinnacle Books, Bristol, 1981, p. 45.

Photo by Robert Alexander

The uprights of the free-standing trilithons were placed so closely together that it is not possible for a man to walk between them.

138

The Moonrise Trilithon is awesome in its symetry and workmanship. The view through the slot reveals the distant horizon.

Photo by Robert Alexander

The stones of the Sarsen Circle were placed with mathematical preci-
sion around a circle whose mean circumference is 316.8 feet—the
number which bears the name Lord Jesus Christ.

7

The Marriage of the Circle and the Square

Male and female are fundamental opposites, yet the sacrament of marriage is a union of these opposites, producing (ideally) one harmonious whole. It is a union ordained of God. I call it a sacrament because it is indeed a sign—an illustration of a greater union. The ultimate union is the oneness between man and his Creator. The thread of the story of this ultimate oneness is woven through all of his dealings with his human creation.

The tracing of the story reveals a most remarkable illustration—the marriage of the circle and the square. I shall use this figure—the circle and the square—to test and amplify the concepts thus far presented.

True science calls for certain logical procedures. During the process of data collecting, inductive reasoning leads to the formation of one or more tentative hypotheses. Epistemology, the study of the origins of knowledge, requires the scientific method of proper investigation of the sources of information during the data collecting period. This begins with observation, description, and the assembling of quantitative data. At this point preconceptions are always present concerning the phenomena being observed—a process of inductive reasoning.

Next is isolation of the parts, or evidences. This requires separation and analysis.

After collecting, isolating and analyzing the available data, deductive reasoning can then enter the picture, and logical thought processes, based upon the analysis of the data begins to formulate a positive hypothesis. These logical consequences must then be tested. If the test results are positive, it is then reasonable to assume that the hypothesis is accurate.

Thus far we have been observing the collected data and indulging the senses in the exiting, mind-blowing processes of inductive reasoning, formulating a hypothesis. These observations have all pointed to a logical conclusion, and a beautiful and harmonious picture begins to emerge. The picture speaks of a Creator who had a definite plan, and carefully and systematically carried out that plan, recording in advance its components and its concepts, building the witnesses of that plan into his material creation. The plan involves the ultimate reconciliation of his human family to himself in an everlasting union.

We have observed many of the witnesses of that plan in the construction and geometry of the Great Pyramid, Stonehenge, the Temple, and the earth, sun and moon. Conclusions have been suggested, that the Creator of the universe was indeed the Architect of these edifices, and that they tell of a redeemer, Jesus Christ, through whom is promised a resurrection from the death condition, and an opportunity for man to return to a condition of harmony with God.

Let's look at some of the evidences which at first glance may seem unrelated, yet, upon closer examination fit into one harmonious whole, piecing together a beautiful picture. The relationship of the circle and the square is the tie that binds the pieces together.

The ancient Hebrew scriptures tell a most revealing story regarding the first human pair, a man and woman made in the *"image and likeness"* of God, a human couple, made in perfection. The story reveals the tragic results of their disobedience to their Creator and their fall from that perfection. The penalty placed upon them for their disobedience was death—not immediate death, but a dying existence in which they were estranged from God.

But they were given a promise of eventual re-union with their Creator, a return to the oneness that they had originally enjoyed.

THE MARRIAGE OF THE CIRCLE AND THE SQUARE

The means by which this re-union could be made possible would be through a redeemer—one to pay the penalty for their disobedience and set them free from their condemnation. Such a redeemer would have to be a substitute, to take their place in death, providing them an opportunity for life. As a surety for the promise of a redeemer, God killed an animal and used its skin to clothe them.

Unto Adam also and to his wife did the Lord God make coats of skins, and clothed them. (Genesis 3:21)

It was no coincidence that the gematria for *"coats of skins,"* כתנות עור, is 288. As we have seen, the magnificent number 288 defines the perimeter of the Great Pyramid and Stonehenge. And a square with sides of 288 has a perimeter of 1152, which is the number for Kingdom of God.

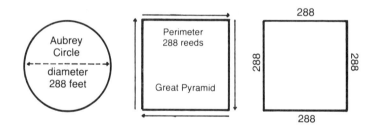

one side 288 — Coats of skins, כתנות עור, 288
perimeter 1152 — Kingdom of God, την βασιλειαν Θεου, 1152

Hidden in the transaction of providing them with coats of skins, God pointed all the way down through seven millennia to his completed kingdom in which Adam and the whole human race would be united once again with their Creator in oneness—a marriage of that which had been fundamental opposites, a marriage illustrated by the union of the circle and the square.

The Apostle John saw a vision of that marriage. He recorded what he saw in these words:

143

And I John saw the holy city, the New Jerusalem, coming down from God out of heaven, prepared as a bride adorned for her husband. And I heard a great voice out of heaven saying, Behold, the tabernacle of God is with men, and he will dwell with them, and they shall be his people, and God himself shall be with them, and be their God. And God shall wipe away all tears from their eyes; and there shall be no more death, neither sorrow, nor crying, neither shall there be any more pain; for the former things are passed away. (Revelation 21:2-4)

The effect of this marriage, as John revealed, is oneness between man and his Creator, and everlasting life.

The correlation of Stonehenge and the New Jerusalem beautifully illustrates the marriage of the circle and the square. When these two geometric figures are brought together in commensurable proportions they are found to contain the same magnificent numbers.

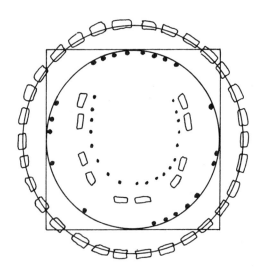

FIGURE 25

THE MARRIAGE OF THE CIRCLE AND THE SQUARE

The ground plan of the New Jerusalem is found to be identical (on a reduced scale) to Stonehenge, the square of its perimeter bearing the same number as the Sarsen Circle, 3168. The perimeter of the New Jerusalem is 31,680,000 feet, and the mean circumference of the Sarsen Circle is 316.8 feet. Both define the means of man's redemption, the Lord Jesus Christ, Κυριος 'Ιησους Χριστος, 3168. If we bring together the proportions of this circle and square, we find that another circle inscribed within the square would define the dimensions of the Bluestone Circle, *i.e.,* a circumference of 144 royal cubits. John described the New Jerusalem as having a wall of 144 cubits.

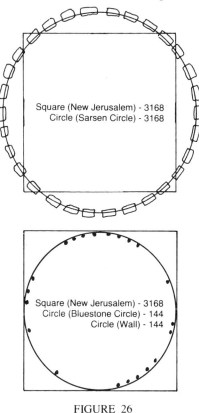

Square (New Jerusalem) - 3168
Circle (Sarsen Circle) - 3168

Square (New Jerusalem) - 3168
Circle (Bluestone Circle) - 144
Circle (Wall) - 144

FIGURE 26

145

THE MAGNIFICENT NUMBERS

The correlation of the magnificent numbers of Stonehenge and the Great Pyramid with the New Jerusalem are listed in detail in *Stonehenge...a closer look* [1] The multiplicity of these number relationships shows a beautiful design by the Creator to illustrate the ultimate unity between himself and his human family. This unity, and the means of its accomplishment, has been written for us in symbol, in story, and in stone. And the incredible truth is that the magnificent numbers tell the story of man's redemption.

The evidences of this plan of redemption are like pieces of a puzzle. The pieces have been hidden, but the search for them is an exciting adventure. And when all the pieces are brought together, and placed in their proper order, a beautiful picture emerges.

The pieces of this ancient puzzle are not to be found in any one place. Many of the pieces are indeed at the Great Pyramid, and many are at Stonehenge. Pieces have been found in the earth, sun, and moon. Some of the pieces have been found in the very foundation of Israel's beautiful Temple; but the search goes on.

Just as the computer provided Professor Hawkins with some of the pieces of the puzzle regarding Stonehenge, so the Bible has proven to be a key to unlock the hiding place of other pieces.

From the evidence thus far presented, we have shown that the architect of both Stonehenge and the Great Pyramid is indeed man's Creator. Thus the Bible is a logical place to look for pieces of the puzzle.

Noah's Ark

1656 years after the disobedience of the first human pair, the corruption of the race had become so intense that they were destroyed in the great flood catastrophe. The family of Noah (8 people), however, were carried through, saved from the certain

---

[1] Bonnie Gaunt, *Stonehenge...a closer look,* Bell Books, Crown Publishing Co., New York, 1982, pp. 131-136.

death by means of a boat. The Bible called it an ark, which really was a rectangular box, built especially to float. The ark was, in fact, the means of salvation to all those inside. The Apostle Peter spoke of the ark as representing the salvation that all humankind receive through the Lord Jesus Christ, (I Peter 3:20, 21).

In fact, hidden in the statement that Peter made is the number 888, which is the gematria for Jesus. He said *"...an ark, in which a few, that is, eight souls were saved through water..."* κιβωτου εις ην ολιγοι τουτ εστιν οκτω ψυχαι διεσωθησαν δι υδατος, 8880. [2]

The dimensions of the ark were 300 cubits long by 50 cubits wide by 30 cubits high. The identification of the cubit is not given, and evidence of what cubit was in use at that time is not available. Rev. John McClintock, D.D., and James Strong, S.T.D., (*Cyclopaedia of Biblical, Theological and Ecclesiastical Literature,* Vol. VII, p. 147) suggest a cubit of 21 inches for the ark. This is a fraction shorter than the great cubit of 21.12 inches. If the great cubit is the correct one, it reveals the remarkable evidence of the British mile unit, for the length of the ark would be exactly the 10th part of a mile, or 528 feet. The height would be the 100th part of a mile, or 52.8 feet. The width would bear the number that represents man's Redeemer, 88 feet. It is likely that this was indeed the unit used, for evidence has been shown that the great cubit played an important role in the construction of the Great Pyramid, built 333 years after, and of Stonehenge, built 500 years after.

The saving of Noah and his family is a fitting picture of the salvation of the whole human race through Jesus Christ.

When they came out of the ark at the cessation of the flood, God established a covenant with them, that he would never again bring a flood of water to destroy all mankind. The token of the covenant was the rainbow that appeared in the cloud. The Genesis record of the event says:

---

[2]This is the literal translation from the Greek. The sentence has been turned around in our English Bibles.

THE MAGNIFICENT NUMBERS

I establish my covenant with you, and with your seed after you; and with every living creature that is with you...neither shall all flesh be cut off any more by the waters of a flood; neither shall there any more be a flood to destroy the earth.... This is the token of the covenant...I do set my bow in the cloud and it shall be a token of a covenant between me and the earth. (Genesis 9:9-13)

How thrilling to find that the promise *"I will establish my covenant,"* והקמתי אתבריתי, has the number value of 1584—a magnificent number indeed. A square drawn on the Bluestone Horseshoe has a perimeter of 1584 feet. And a square with sides of 1584 has a perimeter of 6336, the number of inches in the length of the ark.

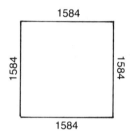

One side, 1584
Perimeter, 6336
Length of Ark, 6336 inches

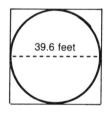

Diameter of Bluestone Horseshoe, 39.6 feet
Perimeter of square, 1584 feet
I establish my covenant, והקמתי אתבריתי,1584

THE MARRIAGE OF THE CIRCLE AND THE SQUARE

If the cubit of Noah's ark is indeed the great cubit, other interesting relationships become apparent. The width of the ark in British inches would be 1,056. It will be remembered that 10.56 feet is the length of the reed (6 great cubits), as well as being the length of the lintels which topped the Sarsen Circle. It is also the number that defines the diameter of the outer face of the Sarsen Circle (105.6 feet) as well as the Bluestone Circle (105.6 yards = perimeter of a square drawn on the Bluestone Circle).

The length of the ark was six times its width. Thus the geometric proportion of its floor is six squares of 88 feet per side. Each square measures 352 feet in perimeter, and when multiplied by 6, gives a total of 2,112. The significance of the number is apparent.

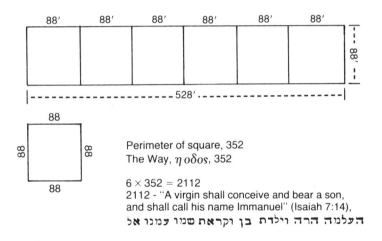

Perimeter of square, 352
The Way, $\eta\ o\delta os$, 352

$6 \times 352 = 2112$
2112 - "A virgin shall conceive and bear a son, and shall call his name Immanuel" (Isaiah 7:14),
העלמה הרה וילדת בן וקראת שמו עמנו אל

When we define the square by the megalithic mile, each side measures .00611 of a MMi. As has been shown in chapter 5, the Biblical references to the topstone of the Great Pyramid are metaphorically speaking of Jesus. The prophet Isaiah referred to him as *"a tried stone, a precious cornerstone,"* (Isaiah 28:16), בחן אבן יקר פנה אבן, which, by gematria, bears the number 611.

THE MAGNIFICENT NUMBERS

A square inscribed within a circle whose diameter is 864 (the solar number) has sides of 611 and a perimeter of 2444.

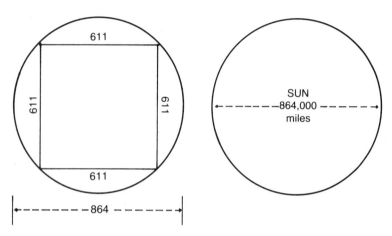

Each side 611 — "A tried stone, a precious cornerstone,"
611 ,בחן אבן יקר פנה אבן

Perimeter 2444 — "The Lord your God," $K\upsilon\rho\iota o\varsigma\ o\ \Theta\epsilon o\varsigma\ \upsilon\mu\omega\nu$,2444
Diameter of sun, 864,000 miles

The ark that saved Noah and his family from death is a figure of something far greater—a Redeemer who saves the human family from Adamic death. The work of redemption is beautifully shown by the circle and the square—two fundamental opposites, yet they foretell a union, a harmony, between man and his Creator!

The Bethel Rock

Rocks play an important role in the story of the salvation of man.

There is a rock that seemingly gets little attention by most students of the Old Testament, yet it became very important to the survival of the Hebrew people. This rock concerns Jacob, the son of Isaac, and the grandson of Abraham.

While fleeing from the wrath of his brother, Esau, Jacob made camp for the night in the desert. As was the custom, he took stones and arranged them in order upon which to place his bedding, thus raising his head to a comfortable position for sleeping. And as he slept that night, he dreamed. In his dream he saw what he called a ladder, probably more like a staircase, which reached from earth to heaven. He saw angels ascending and descending on this staircase, and at its glorious top he saw what appeared to be Jehovah.

Then this glorious being began to speak. He repeated the covenant that had been given to Abraham—*"in thee and in thy seed shall all the families of the earth be blessed."* Following this, he reassured Jacob that he would lead him and eventually bring him back to his homeland.

Upon hearing the confirming of the covenant, Jacob awoke. His first reaction was fear. He said, *"How dreadful is this place! This is none other but the house of God, and this is the gate of heaven."*

Awed by the sublime majesty of the Holy One he had just seen, and stirred in his inner nature by the grandeur of the heavenly vision, he took the stone upon which his head had rested, and set it up for a pillar. He anointed it with oil and called it Bethel, which means *"the house of God."* And as he bowed before this altar-pillar, he made a vow to Jehovah:

If God will be with me, and keep me in this way that I go, and will give me bread to eat, and raiment to put on, so that I come again to my father's house in peace; then shall the Lord be my God: and this stone, which I have set for a pillar, shall be God's house ....

The stone that he had used for a pillow had taken on a new and special meaning. It was now a symbol of the covenant—a covenant that promised a blessing to *"all the families of the earth."* Thus it is not surprising to find that the gematria for this stone points to the means whereby the blessing can become an accomplished fact. The phrase *"and the stone shall become the house of God,"* והאבן יהיה בית אלהים has the number value of 592. A square with sides of 592 has a perimeter of 2368, which is the number for Jesus Christ, 'Ιησους Χριστος.

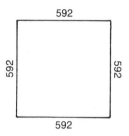

One side, 592 — "and the stone shall become the house of God
והאבן יהיה בית אלהים, 592
Perimeter, 2368 - Jesus Christ, 'Ιησους Χριστος,2368

The Rev. J. H. Allen has suggested[4] that the Bethel stone later became the possession of the descendents of Joseph, and was carried with them during the wilderness wanderings of the people of Israel. He further suggested that this rock was the one from which God caused water to flow, providing drink for the Israelites in the desert.

The first mention of no water for the people to drink was while the Israelites were encamped at Rephidim. Without previously selecting one special rock, the Lord said to Moses: "I will stand before thee there upon *the rock* in Horeb, and thou shalt smite *the rock*, and there shall come water out of it." The phrase "There in Horeb," points out the place where the rock was at the time, and if the Lord when he spoke of the rock, had used the demonstrative form, and said "that rock," then we should know that he was designating which one, or a certain one not yet selected, but the fact that he said "the rock" is proof to us

[4]J. H. Allen, *Judah's Sceptre and Joseph's Birthright*, Destiny Publishers, Haverhill, MA, 1902, pp. 238-240.

that he was speaking of a rock with which they were already familiar. May it not have been the Bethel pillar rock, "the shepherd, the stone of Israel," which had been committed to the keeping of the house of Joseph. [5]

The first mention of obtaining water from the rock may give the appearance that it was a rock native to the area, and perhaps permanently a part of the terrain. However, many years later, Moses was again told to obtain water from the rock, and in this account of the incident, it becomes apparent that the rock was familiar to them.

> *And the Lord spake unto Moses, saying: Take the rod, and gather the assembly together, and speak ye unto the rock before their eyes; and it shall give forth his water, and thou shalt bring forth to them water out of the rock.... And Moses and Aaron gathered the congregation together before the rock...and Moses lifted up his hand, and with his rod he smote the rock twice; and the water came out abundantly, and the congregation drank, and their beasts also.* (Numbers 20:5-11)

Allen's comment on this shows the reasonableness of the concept that the rock was one which was already well-known to them:

> ...although the phrase "the rock" is used four times, there is not the slightest indication that there was any selection, or indication of preference for a certain rock in the vicinity of Kadish, or that one was not already chosen, and in their midst. It was to show also that at the very first mention of water for the people from *"the rock,"* all that was necessary, as a preparatory measure, was for the Lord to say to Moses, "Speak to the rock," and also that when the people were commanded to "gather before *the rock,*" they understood so well which rock it was that, in all that vast company of two and a half millions, no explanations were

---

[5] *Ibid.,* p. 238

necessary. Hence it must have been among them before this, and well known. Let us also bear in mind that this name, *"The Rock,"* was used in the same relation at Rephidim, and yet the children of Israel had removed, journeyed and pitched their tents twenty-one times after leaving Rephidim, and here in Kadesh there is with them that which is still familiarly known as *"THE ROCK."* [6]

Allen's logic is not, however, conclusive. There are other clues which must be examined. The Apostle Paul mentioned this incident of water flowing from the rock, and his language seems to make it clear that the rock was part of their possessions which accompanied them on their journey through the desert.

And all did drink the same spiritual drink; for they drank of that spiritual Rock that followed them; and that Rock was Christ."

The word "followed" is from the Greek $\alpha \kappa o \lambda o \upsilon \theta \epsilon \omega$, which literally means "to be in the same way with" or "to accompany."

Paul not only settled the matter that the rock was portable, and went with them, he also informed us of its symbolism—it represented Christ. Why? Because it was a means of salvation to the Israelites; otherwise they would have died of thirst in the desert. Thus it is fitting that the gematria for Saviour, מושיע, is 426, and the number value for *"water out of the rock,"* ומים נסלע, is also 426, showing that the rock was indeed a symbol of the Saviour.

But conclusive evidence has not been brought forth to prove that the Bethel stone, which symbolized the covenant to bless *"all the families of the earth,"* is indeed one and the same as the rock that they carried with them in the desert, which symbolized salvation through Christ.

Some interesting relationships develop, however, when we consider the gematria of the subjects involved. The number

---

[6] *Ibid.*, p. 240

154

value for *"water from the rock,"* ומים מסלע (Nehemiah 9:6), is 296. It is one of the magnificent numbers already noted as pertaining to Jesus (Son of Man = 2960, Only Begotten = 296, eternal salvation = 2960) thus the fact that it is represented by water from the rock is in perfect harmony with that of which it is indeed a symbol. And the relationship to the Bethel stone is striking! The number value for *"the stone shall become the house of God,"* והאבן יהיה בית אלהים, is 592. A square with sides of 592 has a perimeter of 2368, which is the number for Jesus Christ.

This relationship can best be shown graphically by the following figure:

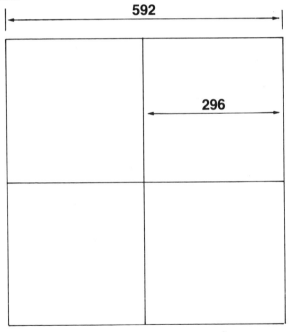

One side of small square, 296 — "water from the rock, ומים מסלע, 296
One side of large square, 592 — "the stone shall become the house of God,
והאבן יהיה בית אלהים, 592
Perimeter of large square, 2368 — Jesus Christ, ’Ιησους Χριστος, 2368

FIGURE 27

THE MAGNIFICENT NUMBERS

As I have mentioned, the concept of the marriage of the circle and the square brings together into a harmonious unity that which had been fundamental opposites. Man, because of the disobedience of Adam, had become estranged from God—the one being sinful, the other being perfect. But the price for the sin of Adam was fully paid by the death and resurrection of Jesus; thus providing the means of bringing man once again into a harmonious relationship with his Creator. We might say that the death of Jesus provided the means whereby the marriage of the circle and the square can become a beautiful reality.

The marriage of the circle and the square is shown graphically by a circle and a square of the same perimeter. The line which defines the outer boundaries is the same length, but in one it takes the shape of a square, and in the other it is shaped as a circle. Using this simple geometric principle, let us observe the gematria involved in 1) the Bethel rock, 2) the rock from which water flowed, and 3) the means of our salvation, Jesus Christ. The harmony of their numerical relationship bears unmistakable testimony that they are parts of a whole—a complete concept.

I show below the graphic progression of this harmonious figure.

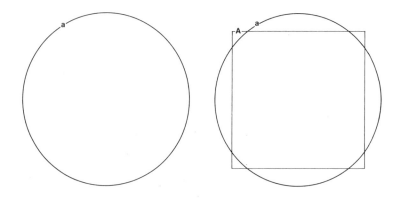

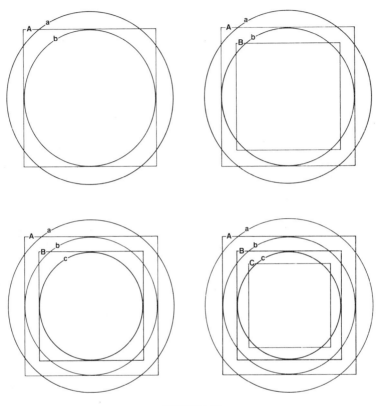

FIGURE 28

The gematria for Jesus Christ is 2368, therefore let us use that figure as the number of units in the circumference of Circle a. Starting with this dimension, by simple mathematics the dimension of the other circles and squares can be obtained. In doing this, the significant numbers begin to appear—numbers relating to the Bethel stone, to the rock from which Moses obtained water, to Jesus Christ, and to the place of his death, Golgotha.

Thus the uniting of the circle and the square brings these into a harmonious relationship. They are telling the story of the confirming of the covenant to Jacob that *"all the families of the earth''* would be blessed; the means of that blessing would be through the Lord Jesus Christ, as was pictured by the life-preserving water that flowed from the rock.

Share with me the thrill and the joy of these relationships. Our God is telling us something great and beautiful and profound!

236.8 - Square A and Circle a
2368 - Jesus Christ, Ἰησους Χριστος

186.0 - Square B and Circle b
186 - Great Rock, סלע כבד (Isaiah 32:2)
186 - Golgotha, Γολγοθα

146.0 - Square C and Circle c
146 - Jehovah-nissee, יהוה נסי (Exodus 17:15)
1460 - *a precious cornerstone, a sure foundation,*
פנת יקרת מוסד מוס ד (Isaiah 28:16)

59.2 - one side of Square A
59.2 - diameter of Circle B
592 - *and the stone shall become the house of God,*
והאבן יהיה בית אלהים (Genesis 28:22, The Bethel stone)

29.6 - radius of Circle b
296 - *water from the rock,* ומים מסלע (Nehemiah 9:6)
296 - rock, רוצ
2960 - eternal salvation, σωτηριας αιωνιου (Hebrews 5:9)
2960 - Son of Man, ο υιος ανθρωπου
296 - Only Begotten, μονογενη

A square drawn tangent to Circle a (not shown in the diagram), would have a perimeter of 301. Again how beautifully it ties together the rock, Jesus, and the place of his death:

301 - *He is the rock,* הצור (Deut. 32:4)
301 - Calvary, κρανιον

The relationship of Circle b to Circle a in this diagram is precisely the relationship of the Sarsen Circle to the Bluestone Circle at Stonehenge. The concept of the marriage of the circle and

the square—the ultimate oneness between man and his Creator—
was built into those ancient stone circles. I do not believe it to
be a coincidence. I believe we have sufficient evidence, at this
point in the investigation, to say with assurance that it was the
plan of the divine Architect, placed there 4,000 years ago as a
witness, and still standing today.

The other stone witness, the Great Pyramid, is in beautiful
geometric harmony with the marriage of the circle and the square.
Using the above diagram, let us consider the diameter of Circle
c as the base of a pyramid—a pyramid whose proportions are that
of the Great Pyramid, having an angle from base to apex of 51°
51'.

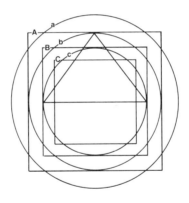

FIGURE 29

The apex of that pyramid would be tangent to Square A. And
using the same units as above, the vertical distance from base to
apex would be 29.6 units. As has been shown, 296 is a number
that relates to the redemption of man. *"For God so loved the
world that he gave his only begotten son,"* (John 3:16); the
gematria for *"only begotten"* is 296; and the gematria for *"eternal salvation"* is 2960. How fitting that the topstone of the

Pyramid, which represents Jesus Christ, rests on the perimeter of Square A whose measure is 2368 units—the number of his name.

The marriage of the circle and the square is not only shown in its relationship to Stonehenge and the Great Pyramid, but also in its relationship to the earth and moon. Using the same diagram, the dimensions of the earth and moon can be drawn on the circles as shown below.

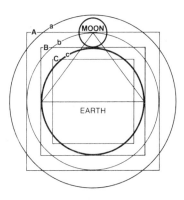

FIGURE 30

Surely the Architect of these orbs was building one great harmonious design—a design that tells the story of the redemption of man and his oneness with his Creator! When Pythagoras discovered that "numbers are the language of the universe" he was touching the very core of creation and the heart of the plan of God.

If Figure 27, shown on page 155, were divided one time the units would be 148. And it will be remembered that 1480 is the gematria for Christ, Χριστος. Divide it one more time and the basic unit is 74, the very foundation of all creation. The word foundation, יסד has a number value of 74. But the number 74 relates to the Creator himself, for it is also the gematria for *"a great God,"* אל גדול.

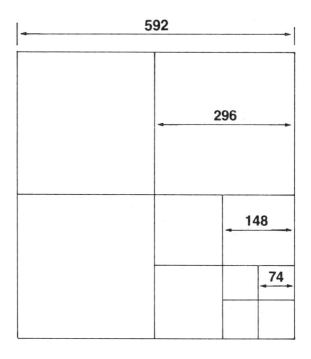

FIGURE 31

These symbols were given by God as a witness of his plan for the redemption of his human family. The word *witness,* עד, has a number value of 74.

I have no hesitation in suggesting that 74 is the very foundation of creation, for the word *creation, κτισις,* has the number value of 740. The word *everlasting,* עד, is 74, and the word *circle, κυκλος,* is 740. A circle indeed represents that which is everlasting—it represents the Creator himself. He is the foundation, the Architect of all creation.

161

The Serpent of Copper

During the experiences of their wilderness journey, the Israelites found themselves in the midst of an area infested with poisonous snakes. Many of the people were bitten and had died.

The setting provided just the right ingredients to picture the greatest event in the history of man.

God instructed Moses to make a serpent of copper and place it on a high pole. Anyone who had been bitten by a poisonous snake could then look upon this copper serpent and be healed. The scripture reads:

And Moses made a serpent of brass (copper) and put it upon a pole, and it came to pass, that if a serpent had bitten any man, when he beheld the serpent of brass, he lived." (Numbers 21:9)

The symbol intended might have remained obscure had not Jesus told us that it pictured his being lifted up on the cross to die.

As Moses lifted up the serpent in the wilderness, even so must the Son of Man be lifted up: that whosoever believeth in him should not perish, but have eternal life. For God so loved the world, that he gave his only begotten Son, that whosoever believeth in him should not perish, but have everlasting life. (John 3:14-16)

But why would God use such a universally hated and feared creature as a serpent to picture his beloved, only begotten Son?

When sin entered the Garden of Eden it entered in the form of a serpent. Its entrance brought death to the human family. Jesus became a substitute for Adam, that Adam and the human family might thereby be freed from the death penalty. The Apostle Paul said *"...he hath made him to be sin for us, who knew no sin; that we might be made the righteousness of God in him."* (II Cor. 5:21)

He was the means of our reconciliation with God because he took the sinner's place. Thus he was prefigured as a serpent, the personification of sin. Therefore it is most appropriate that the

162

gematria for serpent, and the gematria for Messiah should bear the same number—358.

358 - Serpent, נחש

358 - Messiah, משיח

A serpent and a lamb appear to be fundamental opposites; whereas the one is aggressive and deadly, the other is meek, gentle and harmless. Yet these opposites, the serpent and the Lamb of God, come together in simple harmony in the marriage of the circle and the square.

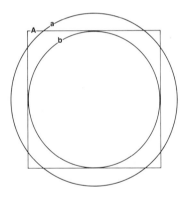

Circumference of Circle a, 358 —Serpent, נחש , 358
Messiah, משיח, 358

Circumference of Circle b, 281 — Lamb, $\alpha\varrho\nu\iota o\nu$, 281

The bringing together of the serpent illustration and the lamb illustration into one harmonious picture is in keeping with the fact that Jesus called his own crucifixion the *"serpent lifted up,"* while Isaiah prophesied of the same event and said *"He is brought as a lamb to the slaughter, and as a sheep before her shearers is dumb, so he opened not his mouth."* (Isaiah 53:7)

The relationship of Circle a to Circle b is precisely the relationship of the Sarsen Circle to the Bluestone Circle. The reconciliation of man to God must, in some way, be prefigured in those circles.

This reconciliation is effected by the fact that Jesus took the place of sin upon the cross. By this act he became the *"author (cause) of eternal salvation,"* (Hebrews 5:9). The title *"author of eternal salvation,"* $\alpha\iota\tau\iota\circ\varsigma$ $\sigma\omega\tau\eta\varrho\iota\alpha\varsigma$ $\alpha\iota\omega\nu\iota\upsilon$, bears the number 3552. A circle with a diameter of 355.2 has a circumference of 1116, which is the number value for *"a serpent of copper,"* נחש נחשת (Num. 21:9).

> *...he became the author of eternal salvation unto all them that obey him; called of God, a high priest after the order of Melchisedec.* (Hebrews 5:9 & 10)

The result of this reconciliation will be peace—world peace, peace with God, and peace within.

Salem (peace) has the number value of 279 ($\Sigma\alpha\lambda\epsilon\mu$). How fitting that a square with sides of 279 has a perimeter of 1116, *a serpent of copper,* נחש נחשת.

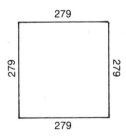

One side, 279 — Salem (peace), $\Sigma\alpha\lambda\epsilon\mu$, 279
Perimeter, 1116 — A serpent of copper, נחש נחשת, 1116

Salem in Hebrew is שלם, 370. It will be noted that a square with sides of 370 has a perimeter of 1480, which is the number value for Christ, Χριστος, 1480.

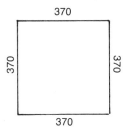

One side, 370 — Salem (peace), שלמ, 370
Perimeter, 1480 — Christ, Χριστος, 1480

Cities for Refuge

After forty years of nomadic life in the wilderness, the Israelites finally came into possession of the land that their God had promised to them. Before entering the land, God gave instruction to Moses regarding the dividing of the territories among the twelve tribes. Because Joseph's tribe had been divided into two tribes (Ephraim and Manasseh) there were now thirteen divisions; however, the property inheritances were divided only into twelve parts. The tribe of Levi received no land.

A greater provision was made for the Levites. They were to be the priestly tribe, and serve as ministers of God's care over the people. The Levites, however, still had to have homes in which to live, therefore God instructed Moses to appoint 48 cities for them.

Of these 48 cities, six were set apart as a special assylum for the accidental manslayer—a place of refuge for anyone who had committed involuntary manslaughter. These six cities were called cities of refuge.

If a resident of any of the appointed twelve territories had ac-

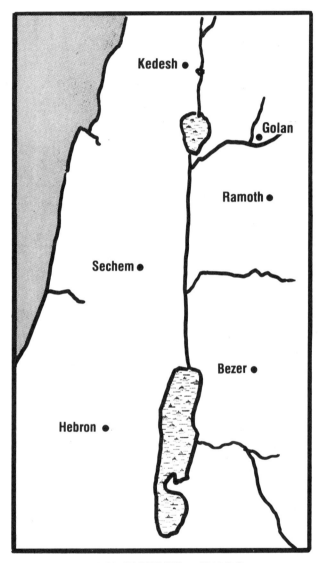

CITIES OF REFUGE, c. 1600 B.C.

cidentally caused the death of any person, he or she could flee to one of the cities of refuge and be safe from the avenger. The manslayer must remain within the protection of the city of his refuge until the death of the high priest, after which he was free to return to his homeland without fear of his avenger.

Adam Clarke made the following observation regarding the purpose for the cities of refuge:

> ...probably intended to typify that no sinner can be delivered from his banishment from God, or recover his forfeited inheritance, till Jesus Christ, the great high priest, had died for his offenses, and risen again for his justification. [7]

The analogy is a fitting one. The scriptures not only describe Jesus as the great high priest, but also indicate that he will have others, a priestly class, to share with him in this great work of effecting the reconciliation of the human family to God. One such reference to this is found in Revelation 20:6:

> *Blessed and holy is he that hath part in the first resurrection...they shall be priests of God and of Christ, and shall reign with him a thousand years.*

This kingly priesthood will function during earth's great millennium. It is the only means of mankind's refuge from Adamic death. The cities of refuge beautifully illustrate this means of man's release from the death curse, and their ultimate reconciliation to God.

The cities of refuge were to be laid out as a square within a square, the inner square being the city, and the outer square the suburbs, pasture, gardens, etc. Each side of the suburbs measured 4,000 cubits, giving a perimeter of 16,000 cubits, while the city had sides of 2,000 cubits, with a perimeter of 8,000 cubits.

The Bible does not indicate which cubit was in use. We must go elsewhere to identify it. A cubit that is known to have been in use at that time, and in that area, is the Sumerian cubit of 1.65

---

[7] Adam Clarke, *Clarke's Commentary,* Abbington Press, New York, pp. 729-731.

THE MAGNIFICENT NUMBERS

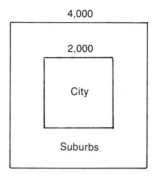

feet, or 19.8 inches. When the dimensions of the city and suburbs are stated in terms of the Sumerian cubit, converted to British inches, the numbers so perfectly illustrate the means of man's salvation and reconciliation, that deductive reasoning indicates it is the correct cubit.

Using the Sumerian cubit, the perimeter of the suburbs would be 316,800 British inches, showing that man's protection is in the Lord Jesus Christ, Κυριος Ιησους Χριστος, 3168. The perimeter of the city would be 158,400 inches, showing the work of reconciliation through the *"priests of God,"* ιερει του Θεου, 1584.

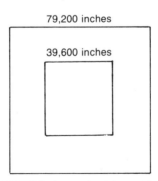

Perimeter of suburbs, 316,800 inches — Lord Jesus Christ,
Κυριος 'Ιησους Χριστος, 3168

Perimeter of city, 158,400 inches — Priests of God, *ιερει του Θεου*, 1584

THE MARRIAGE OF THE CIRCLE AND THE SQUARE

(The perimeter of the suburbs would be five British miles, and the perimeter of the city two and one half miles.)

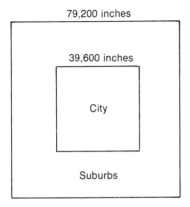

79,200 inches

39,600 inches

City

Suburbs

One side of suburbs
79,200 inches
One side of city
39,600 inches

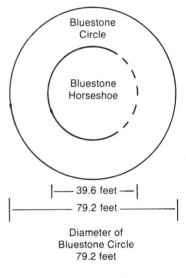

Bluestone
Circle

Bluestone
Horseshoe

|— 39.6 feet —|

|———— 79.2 feet ————|

Diameter of
Bluestone Circle
79.2 feet

Diameter of
Bluestone Horseshoe
39.6 feet

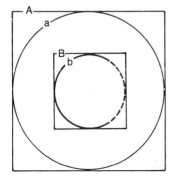

Square A — Suburbs
Square B — City
Circle a — Bluestone Circle
Circle b — Bluestone Horseshoe

(The circles and squares bear the same proportion and the same numbers, but in different units.)

THE MAGNIFICENT NUMBERS

I do not think it is mere coincidence that the relationship of the city to its suburbs is precisely the relationship of the Bluestone Horseshoe to the Bluestone Circle at Stonehenge. Even the numbers involved are the same, but on a reduced scale.

There were six of these cities of refuge, three on each side of the Jordan River. The perimeter of the suburbs of each measures 316,800 inches, which is 26,400 feet. Multiply this by 6 and the total perimeters of the 6 suburbs would be 158,400 feet. Again the number points to the function of the *"priests of God,"* ιερει του Θεου, 1584. The perimeter of each of the cities measured 13,200 feet, and when multiplied by 6 gives a total measure of 79,200 feet. The number 792 is indicative of its complete world-wide function—7920 miles being the diameter of the earth.

When the person involved in involuntary manslaughter fled to the *"city of his refuge,"* and remained within the city, he was delivered out of the hand of the avenger (Numbers 35:25-28). The gematria for *"city of his refuge,"* עיר מקלטו, is 465. A square with sides of 465 has a perimeter of 1860, showing in symbol the place of refuge for the human family, the *Great Rock,* סלע כבד, 186.

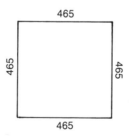

One side, 465 — City of his refuge, עיר מקלטו, 465
Perimeter, 1860 — Great Rock, סלע כבד, 186
Golgotha, Γολγοθα, 186

THE MARRIAGE OF THE CIRCLE AND THE SQUARE

Again the marriage of the circle and the square reveals the beauty of the symbol. Note the same numbers in the figure below as has been shown in figure 28.

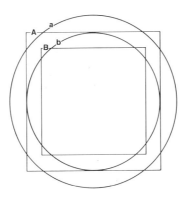

Perimeter of Square A and Circle a, 2368 — Jesus Christ,
'Iησους Xριστος, 2368
One side of Square A, 592 — "and the stone shall become the house of God"
592, והאבן יהיה בית אלהים
Perimeter of Square B and Circle b, 1860 — Great Rock, סלע כבד, 186
Golgotha, Γολγοθα, 186
One side of Square B, 465 — "city of his refuge," עיר מקלטו, 465

The relationship of Circle a to Circle b is identical to the relationship of the Sarsen Circle to the Bluestone Circle. The knowledge of the relationship of these two circles at Stonehenge is not new. It has been mentioned by many who have studied those mysterious stone circles. However, the discovery of their relationship to the plan of God for the salvation of all mankind fills me with awe and wonder, for it is but a brief glimpse into the intricate beauty and the unsearchable riches of the mind of the Creator. The Apostle Paul expressed this feeling in his eloquent words to the early Christians at Rome:

Oh the depth of the riches both of the wisdom and the knowledge of God! How unsearchable are his judgments, and his ways past finding out! For who hath known the mind of the Lord? (Romans 11:33-34)

171

The Great Pyramid bears the same great testimony of a plan of the Creator for the redemption and reconciliation of man. As has been noted, the granite coffer in the King's Chamber has been a silent witness to the resurrection of Jesus Christ. It is silent no longer! Its testimony rings out to all the world, just as the voices of the angels sang to the shepherds on the night of his birth: *"Glory to God in the highest, and on earth peace, and good will to all men."* They were not empty voices. They did not sing a meaningless chorus. They sang of redemption and of the ultimate reconciliation of man to his Creator.

The relationship of the cities of refuge to the granite chamber of the Great Pyramid (the chamber which contained the coffer) further confirms this eloquent testimony.

The *y* circle (365.242) plays an important role in the construction of the King's Chamber and its accompanying Ante-Chamber. The diagram below illustrates this unique feature.

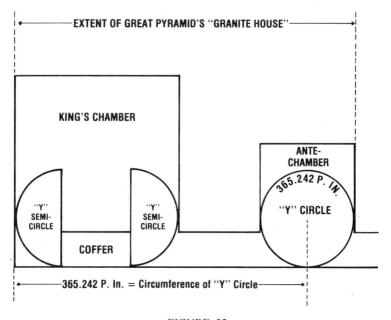

FIGURE 32

172

THE MARRIAGE OF THE CIRCLE AND THE SQUARE

The *y* circle relates to earth's solar year, 365.242 days. This circle which bears such importance in the geometry of the "granite house" of the Pyramid, also plays a vital role in the marriage of the circle and the square, as shown by the diagram below.

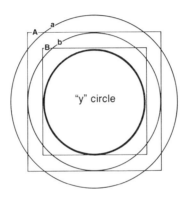

Perimeter of Square A and Circle a, 592 — "the stone shall become the house of God," ‏והאבן יהיה בית אלהים‎, 592

One side of Square A, 148.0 — Christ, $X\rho\iota\sigma\tau os$, 1480

Perimeter of Square B and Circle b, 465 — "city of his refuge," ‏עיר מקלטו‎, 465

Circumference of "y" circle, 365.242

The cities of refuge do indeed provide one more link in the chain of evidence. They tell of the provision made by a powerful, wise, yet loving God, who cared for his human family, and who made ample provision for their release from the Adamic death-curse, and who will ultimately bring them into full reconciliation, harmony and peace with Himself.

Only a few of the beautiful white casing stones remain at the base of the Great Pyramid. These polished white stones once covered its entire surface, causing it to capture and reflect the brilliance of the sun. The enormity of these stones is demonstrated by the arm-span of the man.

8

The Temple in the Vision

The year 597 B.C. was a tragic year for the little nation of Judah, for it was in that year that King Nebuchadnezzar of Babylon came to Jerusalem and took young King Jehoiachin captive, carrying him away to Babylon. Among the Israelite captives was a priest named Ezekiel.

Ezekiel's tragedy was a very personal one. His whole life had been centered in the Temple. He was a man of deep piety and love for God. Having lived this kind of life, centralized about the service of the Temple, he was what we would call today a "misfit" in any other environment. This unified life was rudely snatched away from him by the invasion of Nebuchadnezzar.

Not only was his position of service taken from him, but he was tragically separated from his small children. Nebuchadnezzar had no need of the children; he wanted only the strong, the valiant, the craftsmen and the educated. The children were left behind in Jerusalem, to be cared for by others.

The young man of God, and his wife, were among the large company who made the 700-mile trek across the desert to Babylon. After the wearying three-month journey, they came to a small community near the river Chebar, where they settled.

But the "misfit" Ezekiel mourned for his children and for his communion with God. He had been of the conviction that God could only be found in the Temple. And being separated from the Temple by 700 miles, he felt a lonely separation from God.

After four long years in the land of his captivity he saw the appearance of God in a vision. He saw what seemed to be God riding through the sky in a conveyance apparently propelled by the wings of living creatures and by wheels. The vision was another turning point in his life, for although it frightened and bewildered him, he was overjoyed in that he had seen God in Babylon.

He was now no longer chained to the concept that God dwelled only in the Temple; He could be worshiped in Babylon as well. But the exhilaration which came with the vision was soon accompanied by deep heart-felt grief, for it also told him of the impending doom of his beloved city, Jerusalem, and especially of the beautiful Temple. He was told that the Temple, which had been such a vital part of his life, would soon be destroyed.

The grief deep within his heart was overwhelming. He thought of his children that had been kept in Jerusalem; he thought of the beloved city of his own childhood, and how he longed for it; but most of all he thought of the beautiful Temple, the meeting place between God and man. That it would be destroyed was unthinkable!

Ezekiel was a man of deep conviction. He took upon himself the task of warning his fellow captives that their beloved city and Temple were in danger; but they thought he was just an eccentric visionary, one to be laughed at rather than respected.

In an attempt to convince his peers of the force and impact of what he was telling them, he took a pot and put it on the fire. In the pot he cut up for stew one of the choice of the flock. After cooking the stew, he then completely burned it, replaced the empty pot to the fire and kept it there until its rust and scum had been completely scorched away. It was a symbolic act, depicting the fate of Jerusalem—an act of great impact and significance, for he was caused to write *"Son of man, write thee the name of the day, even this same day; the King of Babylon set himself against Jerusalem this same day."*

But for Ezekiel the tragedy of the day was a very personal one. That day, his wife died.

In one day his grief had reached a height that is hardly possible for a human to bear. His wife had been his only human relationship, for he had been a loner and a misfit. She had been the only one in whom he could find solace for his grief concerning the fate of Jerusalem and the beautiful Temple. They had shared their very personal grief of having left their small children in Jerusalem. Now he was faced with the fact that the city would be destroyed, and it was only natural that his very personal concern would be for the welfare of his children. Such a concern could only be shared by his wife, the mother of his children. And just when he needed her most, she was rudely taken from him. He was left alone with his grief.

News traveled slowly in those days. Six months after the destruction of the Temple, a refugee who had escaped the seige had made his way across the desert to the small community on the river Chebar where Ezekiel lived. He told him of all that had happened, and how the beautiful Temple had been burned with fire. The Temple on the rock, the meeting place between God and man, had been reduced to ashes and rubble.

Was there anything left? Anything at all?

For fourteen long and lonely years in the land of his captivity, Ezekiel mourned the loss of the beautiful Temple—the Temple on the rock. Would there ever again be a meeting place between God and man?

Then one day he had a vision—a vision of a temple whose grandeur and beauty surpassed anything that he had seen or remembered in the Temple he had loved so much. In the vision he saw his God dwelling in that glorious temple; he saw a lovely river of pure water flowing from beneath the temple; and he also saw a beautiful city. In vision he was transported to a high hill, as it were, where he could look down on this spectacular sight.

To Ezekiel it was the confirmation of all that he had lived for—the assurance that God was indeed in the Temple and there was again a meeting place between God and man. To students of the Old Testament, the vision is a promise of redemption from the Adamic death-curse, and a reconciliation to God. It is a beautiful picture of the relationship of man to his Creator during and beyond earth's great millennium.

As we fit the pieces together a beautiful picture emerges, and it is indeed an exciting one, for it confirms the verity of the divine origin of the magnificent numbers.

In the vision Ezekiel saw the appearance of a man with a measuring reed in his hand. *"...and in the man's hand a measuring reed of six cubits long by the cubit and a hand breadth."* (Ezekiel 40:5) [1]

The great cubit was a unit measuring 1.76 feet. Six of these would define the reed of 10.56 feet. As has been shown, each of the perfectly shaped lintels that topped the Sarsen Circle at Stonehenge had a mean length of 10.56 feet. It is a number of beauty and significance, for it identifies the means of salvation, and its effect upon humanity.

"the joy of thy salvation" (Psalm 51:12) שֹשׂון יֹשׁעֶךָ = 1056

The beautiful temple that Ezekiel saw in vision was measured by this unit. Its dimensions speak undeniably of the means of man's salvation—Jesus Christ.

14.08 feet - The porch of the gate, eight cubits (40:9)
1408 - Savior, σωτηρ

3.52 feet - The posts of the porch, two cubits (40:9)
352 - The Way, η οδος

22.88 feet - Length of the gate, thirteen cubits (40:11)
2288 Christ the Lord, Χριστος Κυριος

264 feet - Perimeter of the little chambers, 50 × 25 cubits (40:29)
264 - The Truth, η αληθης

211.2 feet - Perimeter of the porch of the temple, 40 × 20 cubits (41:2)
2112 - *"A virgin shall conceive and bear a son, and shall call his name Immanuel."* (Isaiah 7:14)
העלמה הרה וילדת בן וקראת שמו עמנו אל,

176 feet - Length (and breadth) of temple (41:13, 14)
176 - Counsellor, יועץ (Isaiah 9:6)

The description of the sanctuary, or the Most Holy, (Holy of Holies) of this beautiful temple is outstanding in its numerical

---

[1] See pages 41 through 43 for a description of the great cubit.

relationship to Jesus, the means of man's salvation.

> *...he measured the length thereof, twenty cubits; and the breadth, twenty cubits before the temple; and he said unto me, This is the most holy (holy of holies).* (Ezekiel 41:4)

35.2 feet - Length of Most Holy
35.2 feet - Breadth of Most Holy
352 - The Way, $\eta \, o\delta os$

140.8 feet - Perimeter of Most Holy
1408 - Savior, $\sigma\omega\tau\eta\rho$

10.56 feet - Height of Most Holy
1056 - *"the joy of thy salvation"* (Psalm 51:12) ששון ישעך

The number value for Most Holy in both Greek and Hebrew is 864, $\alpha\gamma\iota\omega\nu$, קדש הקדסים , the solar number, the source of light and life.

The walls, or face of the sanctuary, were carved with the likeness of cherubim and palm trees. Each cherub had two faces—the face of a man and the face of a lion. Thus even the ornamental work spoke symbolically of the means of man's salvation, the *"Son of Man,"* the *"Lion of the tribe of Judah."*

As well as pictorally representing man's redeemer, the face of the sanctuary bore even more significance when we find that its number value is 555.

555 - *the face of the sanctuary,* ופני הקדש

It is a number representative of the divine rulership during earth's great Millennium. This triplet of fives is found in Revelation 11:15 *"The kingdoms of this world are become the kingdom of our Lord and his Christ and he shall reign for ever and ever."* The divine rulership *"our Lord and his Christ,"* $\varkappa\upsilon\varrho\iota\upsilon \, \eta\mu\omega\nu$ $\varkappa\alpha\iota \, \tau\upsilon \, X\varrho\iota\sigma\tau\upsilon \, \alpha\upsilon\tau\upsilon$, has the numerical equivalent of 5550. It is the fulfillment of the prophecy of Isaiah 9:6, 7:

> *The government shall be upon his shoulder; and his name shall be called Wonderful, Counsellor, the Mighty God, the*

Everlasting Father, the Prince of Peace. Of the increase of his government and peace there shall be no end."

The wall surrounding the temple measured 500 great cubits[2] on each side, giving a perimeter of 3,520 feet. How thrilling to realize that the perimeter of this beautiful temple bears the number that describes the way to life— *"I am the Way, the Truth, and the Life."*

> 3,520 feet - Perimeter of the temple
> 352 - The Way, $\eta \, o\delta o\varsigma$

While still in vision, Ezekiel looked down from his vantage point and saw a city to the south, in the portion of land that was set aside as an offering to God. The holy portion was a square measuring 25,000 cubits[2] per side, giving a perimeter of 33.3 miles. This holy offering to God bears the number of His name—God the Saviour, Θεω τω σωτηρι, 3330.

> 33.3 miles - Perimeter of holy portion
> 3330 - God the Saviour, **Θεω τω σωτηρι**

The city Ezekiel saw to the south is commensurate in its measurements with the New Jerusalem, Stonehenge, and the geometry of the earth. It is indeed prophetic of man's complete reconciliation to God—a world-wide condition.

Each side of the city measured 4,500 great cubits, or 7,920 feet. Since the diameter of the earth is 7,920 miles, it is obvious that the city becomes a model of the earth.

Each side of the city was divided into three portions of 2,640 feet each, showing that it is surrounded by and encompassed with truth.

---

[2] See Appendix III, The Cubit vs. Reed of Ezekiel's Vision.

THE TEMPLE IN THE VISION

The perimeter of the city is 18,000 great cubits or 31,680 feet. Thus it is commensurate with the Sarsen Circle at Stonehenge whose mean circumference is 316.8 feet, the New Jerusalem whose perimeter is 31,680,000 feet, and the cities of refuge, (and their suburbs), whose perimeter is 316,800 inches. This perimeter of 31,680 feet illustrates that the Lord Jesus Christ, Κυριος Ἰησους Χριστος, will be its king, for he will be King of kings and Lord of lords. The city is representative of the whole earth, and his number surrounds it, because it belongs to him by right of purchase. He purchased it with his life on Calvary's cross.

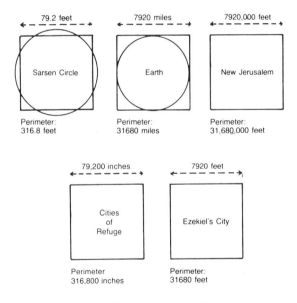

Lord Jesus Christ, Κυριος Ἰησους Χριστος, 3168

This city, whose dimensions are commensurate with the earth, had a name—Jehovah-shammah, which means "the Lord is there." And indeed he is.

371 - Jehovah-shammah, יהוה שמה

THE MAGNIFICENT NUMBERS

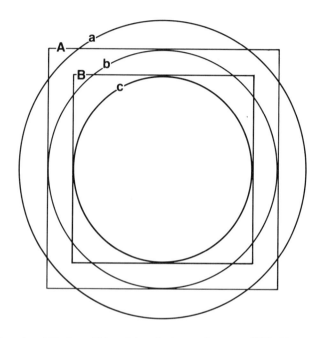

Diameter of Circle a, 371 — Jehovah-shammah, יהוה שמה, 371
Diameter of Circle b, 291 — Earth, ארץ, 291
Diameter of Circle c, 228.8 — Christ the Lord, Χριστος Κυριος, 2288

"The Lord is there"—what a meaningful name! It is descriptive of the completed work of the reconciliation of man to his Creator. A similar description is found in Revelation 21:3 *"The tabernacle of God is with men, and he will dwell with them, and they shall be his people, and God himself shall be with them and be their God."*

"The Tabernacle of God," η σκηνη του Θεου, has the number value of 1584, perfectly corresponding to the "rainbow promise" given to Noah — *"I will establish my covenant,"* את בריתי והקמתי, 1584.

The Apostle John continued his description of the completed work of reconciliation with the beautiful promise:

And God shall wipe away all tears from their eyes; and there shall be no more death, neither sorrow nor crying, neither

182

THE TEMPLE IN THE VISION

shall there be any more pain; for the former things are passed away. (Revelation 21:4)

The city that Ezekiel saw in vision had twelve gates, three on each side. Each was named for one of the twelve tribes of Israel. The number 3168 (Lord Jesus Christ) not only defines the perimeter of the city, it also is the sum of the names of the twelve tribes of Israel.

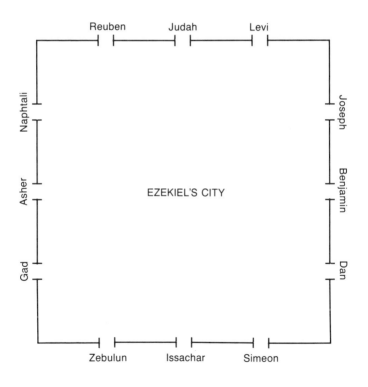

FIGURE 33

Reuben, ראובן	259	
Judah, יהודה	30	
Levi, לוי	46	
Joseph, יוסף	156	
Benjamin, בנימן	152	
Dan, דן	54	(55)
Simeon, שמעון	466	
Issachar, יששכר	830	
Zebulun, זבולן	95	
Gad, גד	7	(8)
Asher, אשר	501	
Naphtali, נפתלי	570	
	3166*	
	(3168)	

While still beholding this remarkable vision, Ezekiel saw movement below. He looked again and realized that water was flowing out from beneath the temple. It flowed eastward, and increased in volume as it went. Then, as if he were in the midst of the stream, he found that at one thousand cubits from the temple the water was up to his ankles. At two thousand cubits it was up to his knees. At three thousand cubits it was to his waist, and at four thousand cubits it was above his head: *"...for the waters were risen, waters to swim in, a river that could not be passed over."* (Ezekiel 47:5)

1,000 cubits	=	1,760 feet
2,000 cubits	=	3,520 feet
3,000 cubits	=	5,280 feet (1 mile)
4,000 cubits	=	7,040 feet

Ezekiel watched while the waters of the river flowed into the Dead Sea, purifying and healing it, making it possible for fish to live in it. Along the banks of the river were trees whose fruit was for food and whose leaves were for medicine.

The Dead Sea has long been used as a picture of the Adamic death-curse. But the waters that flowed from beneath the temple healed the waters of the Dead Sea, making it a "live sea."

---

* In gematria, one or two units known as colel, may be added or subtracted from the value of any word without affecting its meaning.

THE TEMPLE IN THE VISION

664 years after Ezekiel saw this beautiful life-giving river, the Apostle John was given a similar vision. He described it thus:

And he showed me a pure river of water of life, clear as crystal, proceeding out of the throne of God and of the Lamb. In the midst of the street of it, and on either side of the river, was there the tree of life, which bare twelve manner of fruits, and yielded her fruit every month: and the leaves of the tree were for the healing of the nations. " (Revelation 22:1 & 2)

The story of God's magnificent numbers is indeed the story of life—life given and life received. It tells of the greatest gift of all— *"For God so loved the world that he gave his only begotten Son."*

The magnificent numbers reveal the secret, they lay bare the evidence, that the Creator had a plan from the beginning—a plan that would provide life for his beloved human family.

The story of the magnificent numbers touches the lives of every one of us.

This unusual view of Stonehenge was taken along the line of its central axis. The Heel Stone can be seen in the center in the distance. This is the alignment of sunrise on the morning of summer solstice.

Appendix I

The Pyramid Angle

The azimuth of the summer solstice sunrise at Stonehenge
has been given variously, by different authors, as:

49°34'
49°45'
49°47'
49°57'
50°26'
51°13'
51°18'
51°22'
51°30'
51°36'

The controversy goes grandly on! Why? Is not the relative
position of the sun fixed? Yes and no.

In determining the azimuth of the sunrise at the summer
solstice at Stonehenge there are a number of variables, all of
which must be taken into consideration.

1. Because of the tilt of the earth's axis a phenomenon
   known as the precession of the equinoxes causes the sun
   to appear to slip back along the ecliptic. In about 26,000
   years it slides backward one full revolution. Therefore,
   the azimuth of the solstice sunrise in 1973 B.C. would be
   to the left of its present position.

2. What do we consider as sunrise? Is it first flash, half
   disc, or full orb resting tangent to the horizon? From
   first flash to full orb requires about 4 minutes, during
   which time the sun moves nearly one degree to the right.

3. What is the altitude of the horizon? Is it the same today
   as when Stonehenge was built?

4. Does the Heel Stone substitute for the horizon? If so, was it originally placed upright, or leaning at 30° from the perpendicular as it is today?
5. From what height should the sunrise be viewed? Should a six-foot man stand in the Sarsen Center, on the Altar Stone or on the bank behind the Great Central Trilithon?
6. Are refraction and parallax valid considerations? Both affect the apparent position of the sun.

Now that is a lot of variables! And they all must be taken into consideration—not one at a time but all together. The determining of the precise azimuth of sunrise when Stonehenge was built, therefore, appears impossible because of the quantity of unknown essential facts. But is it, in fact, impossible? Is there anything at Stonehenge that would mark it as a fixed position?

The Heel Stone has always been connected with the viewing of the summer sunrise. It was once called the Sunstone for this reason. The name Heel Stone probably comes from the Greek, *helios,* for sun.

A CBS Television Network program "Mystery of Stonehenge" filmed the solstice sunrise at Stonehenge in 1964. The photo shows a little less than half the sun's disc above the peak of the Heel Stone. The precession of the equinoxes has not separated the Heel Stone from the sun, for in 1973 B.C. it appeared on the horizon to the left, but its full orb appeared to be perched atop the Heel Stone. Through nearly 4,000 years the sun still crowns the Sunstone. This is shown by the illustration below.

The permanent position of the Heel Stone becomes a fixed marker for the azimuth of sunrise, unchangeable through time. The use of the Heel Stone for this all-important alignment eliminates all the variables, for the angle from north can be measured on the ground with no need of horizons. It matters not whether the builder placed the Heel Stone upright or tilted toward the center of the monument. Though the actual angle of sunrise-to-north has slowly changed

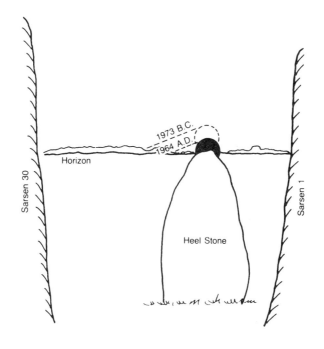

Horizon

Sarsen 30

Sarsen 1

1973 B.C.

1964 A.D.

Heel Stone

FIGURE 34

through time, its permanent marker has remained stationary. A line from the Sarsen Center to the center of the Heel Stone is 51°51′ from north, and it will never change.

Once again we stand in awe of the infinite knowledge and foresight of the builder! What man could have invented a device that would permanently fix the azimuth of sunrise? Yet the builder of Stonehenge did it with a rough unhewn stone!

This angle, 51°51′, is the famous Pyramid angle. It is often called the π angle because it gives to the height of the Great Pyramid the same relation to its square base as the radius of a circle bears to its circumference.

The angle that should permanently mark the sunrise on that remote plain in the British Isles was monumentalized in stone

167 years earlier by the angle of the Great Pyramid on the Gizeh Plateau in Egypt.

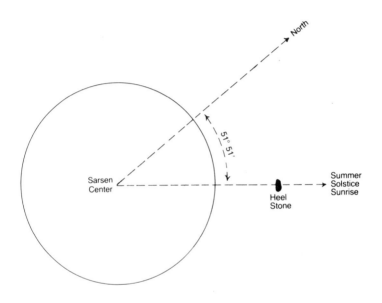

FIGURE 35

Appendix II

The Birth, Baptism and Death of Jesus

The date of Jesus' birth is generally accepted as 4 B.C. It may surprise some to find that no ancient historian, either ecclesiastical or secular, has recorded his birth as being in that year. Erroneous conclusions have been derived from certain statements of the Jewish historian, Josephus—conclusions which his records to not warrant.

Tertullian, one of the early Christian Fathers, born about 160 A.D., stated that Augustus began to rule 41 years before the birth of Jesus and died 15 years after that event. (Tert. adv. Judaeos c. 8) The date of Augustus' death is recorded as August 19, 14 A.D. This would place the birth of Jesus at 2 B.C. (One year is subtracted because there was no zero year between B.C. and A.D.)

In the same chapter, Tertullian stated that Jesus was born 28 years after the death of Cleopatra. Her death is recorded in history as occurring in 30 B.C.; again making the birth of Jesus to be in 2 B.C.

Irenaeus, who was born about a hundred years after Jesus, stated (iii. 25) that "Our Lord was born about the forty-first year of the reign of Augustus." Since Augustus began his rulership in the autumn of 43 B.C., it would place the birth of Jesus in the autumn of 2 B.C.

Eusebius (c. 264-340 A.D.), who was termed the Father of Church History, wrote, "It was the forty-second year of the reign of Augustus and the twenty-eighth from the subjection of Egypt on the death of Antony and Cleopatra" (Eccles. Hist.

i. 5). The 42nd year of Augustus began in the autumn of 2 B.C. and ended in the autumn of 1 B.C. The subjugation of Egypt and its incorporation into the Roman Empire occurred in the autumn of 30 B.C.; therefore the 28th year from that time extended from the autumn of 3 B.C. to the autumn of 2 B.C. Hence the only possible date for the birth of Jesus that would conform to both of these requirements would be the autumn of 2 B.C.

The common acceptance of the 4 B.C. date for the birth of Jesus is based on the oft-repeated statement that the death of Herod the Great was astronomically fixed by Josephus' record of an eclipse of the moon shortly before Herod died; and that eclipse has been shown to have occurred on March 13, 4 B.C.

Even simple reasoning would show the impossibility of the birth of Jesus being in that year, for the Biblical record not only shows his birth to be in the autumn, it shows additionally that considerable time elapsed between Jesus' birth and Herod's death, for the family fled to Egypt to escape Herod's edict that all boy babies should be killed.

The lunar eclipse on March 13, 4 B.C. was a small one (about 4 digits) and was visible in Israel from 2:00 a.m. until about 4:00 a.m. Coming at such an hour it would be noticed by very few people. Josephus was not a recorder of eclipses. In all his writings this is the only eclipse he ever mentioned. Lunar eclipses are common, often happening two or three times in a single year. It is hardly consistent, therefore, that Josephus would mention a small eclipse that happened in the early morning when everyone was asleep, and associate it with the burning of Matthias the day before. Speaking of the burning of Matthias by Herod, Josephus said "And on that very night there was an eclipse of the moon." To comply with the record of Josephus it is reasonable that we look for an eclipse of the moon that was noticeable by its magnitude, and occurred in the early part of the night when people were up to see it. The correct eclipse to which Josephus referred would have to comply with the following requirements:

1) an eclipse not less than two months, but less than six months prior to a Passover,

2) be visible in the early part of the night at Jerusalem,

3) be of sufficient magnitude to be noticeable.

An eclipse that complies perfectly with these requirements occurred on the evening of December 29, 1 B.C., almost exactly three months before the Passover. It was an eclipse of about 7 digits, thus more than half the orb was obscured. The moon was already in eclipse when it rose over Jerusalem that night and continued for about two hours, so that even children would have been able to see it before being put to bed.

Since Herod died shortly after the burning of Matthias but two months before the Passover, his death would have occurred some time in January of 1 B.C. An ancient Jewish scroll, the *Magillath Ta'anith,* written during the lifetime of Jesus, gives the day and month of Herod's death as the 1st of Shebat. The 1st of Shebat in 1 B.C., by the Julian Calendar, would be January 14.

The world celebrates the birth of Jesus on December 25th—Christmas. The early Christian church did not celebrate his birth, thus the exact date was not preserved in tradition and festival observances. The first recorded mention of December 25 is in the calendar of Philocalus (354 A.D.) which showed Jesus' birth to be Friday, December 25, 1 A.D. The date is inconsistent with itself for December 25 of that year was, in fact, a Sunday.

The date of December 25 was officially proclaimed by the church fathers in 440 A.D., and was chosen because it Christianized the pagan festival of the Saturnalia. The winter solstice had meant the diminishing of the sun and its return again. Its central idea, the return of light, became the hope of the world in the birth of Jesus, the light of the world. The transition from paganism to Christianity was gradual, but became generally accepted after the fall of Rome in 476 A.D.

The exact date of Jesus' birth can, however, be determined from the available historical records. The information given in the Bible concerning the time of the conception of John the Baptist furnishes one method of calculation. Elizabeth, the mother of John, was a cousin of Mary and the wife of a priest named Zacharias. Luke 1:5 states that Zacharias was a priest of the course of Abia (Abijah). Verses 8-13 state that while Zacharias *"executed the priest's office before God in the order of his course"* he was given the message that Elizabeth would have a son and that they should name him John. In verses 23 and 24 it is recorded, *"And it came to pass that as soon as the days of his ministration were accomplished, he departed to his own house."*

The priests were divided into 24 classes (I Chronicles 24: 7-19) and each class officiated in the Temple for one week. The courses of the priests changed duty with the change of the week, *i.e.,* from the end of the Sabbath at sundown until the next Sabbath. Both the Talmud and the historian, Josephus, state that the Temple was destroyed by Titus on August 5, 70 A.D., and that the first course of priests had just taken office. The previous evening was the end of the Sabbath. The course of Abia (Abijah) was the 8th course, thus figuring backward we are able to determine that Zacharias ended his course and came off duty on July 13, 3 B.C., and returned home to Elizabeth. The conception of John occurred that weekend (13th-14th) and the birth of John would take place 280 days later, namely April 19th-20th of 2 B.C., precisely at the Passover of that year.

Elizabeth hid herself 5 months, and at the beginning of her 6th month the angel Gabriel appeared to Mary, telling her of Elizabeth's condition. At the same time Gabriel told Mary that she, too, would conceive and bear a son who would be called Jesus. Upon hearing this Mary went *"with haste"* from Nazareth to Ein Karim to visit Elizabeth, who was then in the first week of her 6th month. The time was the 4th week of December, 3 B.C. The 23rd of December of that year, according to the Julian Calendar then in use, was precisely the winter solstice. If this were the date of the conception of Jesus, 280 days later would place the date of his birth at September 29, 2 B.C., *i.e.,* 1st Tishri, the day of the Feast of Trumpets—the Jewish New Year. This day had been set aside in the Law of Moses as a holy day. How fitting that the holy Son of God should be born on that day!

The day on which Jesus was born was not only the first day

of the year but was also the first day of the 77th Sabbatic Cycle since the Jewish return from Babylonian captivity. From the re-establishment of the Sabbatic Cycles in Tishri 534 B.C. till the birth of Jesus in Tishri 2 B.C. was also a great Paschal Cycle of 532 years—a Paschal Cycle being the product of the *Metonic Cycle* (19) and the *Solar Cycle* (28), *i.e.,* 19 x 28 = 532 years.

Luke 3:1 clearly states that John the Baptist began his ministry in the 15th year of Tiberius Caesar. According to the Law of Moses a Jew was considered of age for the ministry at 30 (Numbers 4:3). Augustus had died on August 19, 14 A.D.; thus that year became the accession year of Tiberius, even though he had been involved in and associated with the Roman rulership before Augustus died. If John the Baptist had been born April 19th-20th, 2 B.C., his 30th birthday would be April 19-20, 29 A.D., or the 15th year of Tiberius. Thus the 2 B.C. date for the birth of John is comfirmed by the Biblical record. John was 5 months older than Jesus, making the birth of Jesus to be in the autumn of that year.

That his birth was in the autumn is further confirmed by the prophecy of Daniel (Daniel 9:24-27) which prophesied that there would be 3½ years from Jesus' anointing as the Messiah until his death. If his ministry began when he was 30 (Luke 3:23) and lasted 3½ years, and if he was crucified on the day of Passover (spring), simple arithmetic would show that his birth had to be in the autumn.

The Baptism

The ministry of John began when he was 30 years old in the 15th year of Tiberius, thus Jesus' baptism was also in the 15th of Tiberius, *i.e.,* 29 A.D. Luke 3:23 states that when Jesus was baptized he *"began to be about 30 years of age."* Why the indefinite term *"about?"* Would he not have been very careful to begin his ministry exactly on his 30th birthday? No! It was more important that he fulfill the antitypical significance of his ministry.

The Atonement Day sacrifices of ancient Israel in the Tabernacle were types, or illustrations, of Jesus offering his body in sacrifice for the sins of the world. The Day of Atonement was the 10th day of Tishri. It was fitting therefore, to fulfill the picture, that Jesus offer himself on the Day of Atonement. His *"baptism into death"*—the offering of himself—was on the 10th of Tishri, 29 A.D., which, according to the Julian Calendar, was October 7th.

Did his water baptism, which was the outward or public symbol of his real death baptism, take place on the same day? On first thought it would seem natural to think that it did. Immediately following his water baptism the Biblical record states that he went into the wilderness for 40 days. Had he been baptized on the 10th of Tishri and gone into the wilderness for the next 40 days he would have broken the Law of Moses and sinned, for according to that Law (Deuteronomy 16:16) all Jewish men were required to appear at the Temple at Jerusalem during the days of the Feast of Tabernacles which began 15th Tishri. Assuming that he went to the Temple on the 15th, the whole of the next day would be required for walking to the Jordan. The day following began at sundown, thus the earliest possible day in which Jesus could be baptized and still fulfill all the requirements of the Law would be the 17th of Tishri (October 14, 29 A.D.).

His Death

It is from the prophecy of Daniel that we know the length of Jesus' ministry, *i.e.*, 3½ years. However, the same length of time can be deduced from the fact that he observed four Passovers during his ministry. (John 2:13; 5:1; 6:4; 13:1) He turned 30 in the autumn of 29 A.D. and the observance of four Passovers would reach to the spring of 33 A.D. But what was the exact day of his crucifixion?

From the Biblical record we know that the crucifixion took place on the day of Passover and that it was a Friday. The Passover was always observed on the 14th of Nisan, which in 33 A.D. was a Friday. According to the Mosaic Law the

Passover lambs were to be slain at 3:00 p.m. on Nisan 14. Josephus, who was an eye-witness to the killing of Passover lambs, stated (*Wars* VI, ix, 3) that they began to slay the lambs at the "ninth hour" (Jewish time corresponding to 3:00 p.m.). According to Mark 15:34-38 this was the precise hour that Jesus died on the cross. The Apostle Paul, some years later, explained that Jesus was the antitypical Passover lamb when he said, *"Christ our Passover is slain for us."* (I Corinthians 5:7).

The Passover lambs were always slain on the afternoon of full moon, *i.e.,* when the moon rose that evening it was full. This was because the first day of the month was determined by the observance of the new moon, and full moon always occurs 14 days later. On the afternoon of April 3, 33 A.D. the antitypical Passover Lamb died on a cross atop Golgotha's Hill outside Jerusalem. At 3:06 Greenwich time the moon eclipsed. When the moon rose over Jerusalem that night it was still eclipsed for 17 minutes.

Appendix III

The Cubit vs. Reed of Ezekiel's Vision

The holy portion of land as described in Ezekiel 45:1 and 48:8 appears to be stated as 25,000 reeds in the King James Version; however the word "reeds" is in italic, showing that it has been supplied by the translators. If reeds were the correct unit, it would make the holy portion 50 miles in length, which is not possible because the land between the Mediterranean and the Jordan at that latitude is only about 45 + miles, making the holy portion overlap the available land area on both sides, and leaving no room for the portion for the prince, as described in Ezekiel 45:7 and 48:21. Since the unit is not given in the original Hebrew in these passages, it would appear to be left to the interpreter to determine what unit was meant. Therefore we must look further for evidence.

A careful study of Ezekiel, chapters 42 through 48, reveals the evidence that the unit used for the measure of the temple and the city is also used for measuring the holy portion of land.

According to the King James Version, the temple area is stated in Ezekiel 42:16-20 as being a square with each side of 500 reeds. However in 45:2 the same thing is given as 500 cubits. The obvious contradiction reveals a corruption of the text.

The Revised Standard Version gives the unit as cubits, probably using the Septaugint as the authority for this. The Interpreter's Bible (Abbington Press, Nashville, 1956, vol. 6, pp. 297-338) shows that the reed was the instrument used, but the linear measurement is given in cubits, for both the temple area and the holy portion of land.

The length of the temple area is 500 units. If the unit is the reed, it would render the sides as one mile each. This is an unreal dimension and is vastly out of proportion to all the interior measurements and descriptions. However, if the unit is the cubit, it would render the area as 880 feet per side, which corresponds completely with all the interior dimensions, and is not beyond a reasonable size for the perimeter of the compound.

The evidence leads to the conviction that the holy portion of land was 25,000 cubits per side, or a perimeter of 176,000 feet or 33.3 miles (8.3 miles per side). The temple area was 500 cubits per side, or a perimeter of 3,520 feet (880 feet per side). The city, also given in cubits, would measure 4,500 cubits per side, or a perimeter of 31,680 feet (6 miles).

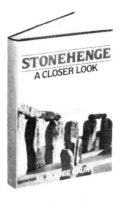

Bibliography

J. H. Allen, *Judah's Sceptre and Joseph's Birthright,* Haverhill, MA, Destiny Publishers, 1902

A. E. Berriman, *Historical Metrology,* London, J. M. Dent & Sons, 1953

Adam Clarke, *Clarke's Commentary,* New York, Abbington Press

Morton Edgar, *The Great Pyramid,* Glasgow, Maclure, Macdonald & Co., 1924
——————— *The Great Pyramid, Its Scientific Features,* Glasgow, Maclure, Macdonald & Co., 1924

Encyclopedia Judaica, Jerusalem, Keter Publishing House, 1972, p.947

Bonnie Gaunt, *Stonehenge...a closer look,* New York, Crown Publishing Co., 1982

Gerald S. Hawkins, *Stonehenge Decoded,* New York, Dell Publishing Co., 1965

Fred Hoyle, *On Stonehenge,* W. F. Freeman and Company, 1977

Jerry Lucas, *Theomatics,* New York, Stein and Day, 1977

John Michell, *City of Revelation,* New York, Ballantine Books, 1972
——————— *Ancient Metrology,* Bristol, Pinnacle Books, 1981

Wm. Flinders Petrie, *Stonehenge, Plans, Description, and Theories,* London, Edward Stanford, 1880

Adam Rutherford, *Pyramidology Book I,* London, Institute of Pyramidology, 1970
——————— *Pyramidology Book II,* London, Institute of Pyramidology, 1962

Joseph A. Seiss, *Miracle in Stone,* Philadelphia, The Castle Press, 1877

Peter Tompkins, *Secrets of the Great Pyramid,* New York, Harper & Row, 1971

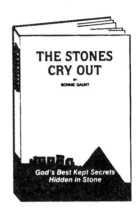